T0315668

Embroidering History:

An Englishwoman's Experience as a Humanitarian Aid Volunteer in Post-War Poland, 1924-1925

Jane Cooper

Embroidering History:

An Englishwoman's Experience as a
Humanitarian Aid Volunteer in Post-War
Poland, 1924-1925

First Published in Great Britain in 2012 by The Derby Book Publishing Company Ltd, 3 The Parker Center, Derby DE21 4SZ

© Jane Cooper, 2012.

All Rights Reserved. No part of this publication may be reproduced, stored in a retrieval system, or transmitted in any form, or by any means, electronic, mechanical, photocopying, recording or otherwise without the prior permission in writing of the copyright holders, nor be otherwise circulated in any form or binding or cover other than in which it is published and without a similar condition being imposed on the subsequent publisher.

ISBN 978-1-78091-143-4

Printed and bound by Copytech (UK) Limited, Peterborough.

Contents

Preface

During September 2011, a few days after reading "Embroidering History", I visited the northern border between Kenya and Somalia, and saw, just like Margaret Tregear had seen 86 years before, a hostile landscape filling up with displaced people, all their possessions gone, with food in chronically short supply. This land was hot and arid: a far cry from the damp and marshy western borders of Belarus where this book is set; but here again was the trauma of displacement, of hunger and of flight from war.

How best to provide assistance to people in extreme need, so that it preserves life and health but also a capacity for economic regeneration, is a challenge that continues to face humanitarian workers to this day. "Embroidering History" shows how Margaret was facing this challenge in the early days of the humanitarian industry, at a time when Europe was still reeling from the impact of its most devastating war, and long before images of immediate suffering could be transmitted to people's homes and stir public outcries.

Like humanitarian workers wrestling with challenges in modern day Horn of Africa, Margaret was involved in what we would now call a "complex emergency". The Russian Empire was being torn apart by civil war, with territories shifting hands, clashes of ideology, a toxic mix of international interference and neglect, mass population movement and famine. As with modern day Somalia, much of the humanitarian support had to take place around the borders.

By the early Twentieth Century, the Russian "intelligentsia" could mix relatively easily across a wider European community, but the vast majority of the population were still illiterate peasants, and to Margaret, they would have seemed exotic and alien. She had to face the divides that all humanitarian workers have to face: that of culture, and that of power.

Power is usually on the side of the aid workers – to administer, to allocate and to withhold resources. This is invariably frustrating for both sides, and triggers arrogance and impatience among the givers, and despondency and passive resistance among the receivers. Decades of sensitisation hasn't rid the humanitarian industry of this dynamic, so it's perhaps not surprising that we find these symptoms in Margaret's letters.

Margaret's letters, which have been so ably edited and put in context here by Jane Cooper, cast light upon the early workings of humanitarian aid, upon population movement across the Russian-Polish border in the 1920s, but also upon a generation of women who broke the mould, and liberated themselves, by choice or necessity, from the stifling expectations of marital roles of that time. This is perhaps the hardest aspect of these letters to appreciate now: just how brave and novel it was for a single woman to embark on an adventure like this.

For those interested in the period and the context, these letters will provide a fresh glimpse into how the two were experienced. For those interested in the evolution of humanitarian aid, despite the time that has passed, the common threads to the present day will be clear.

Alexander Matheou
Regional Representative for East Africa
International Federation of Red Cross and Red Crescent Societies

Dear Friends,

I am inspired this time
To write you all a little rhyme
About the duties manifold
(Some you already have been told)
That must be undertaken by
The worker in this Industry
First, she must know all shapes and sizes,
Cost of production, final prices,
Of every tray cloth, bag and runner,
Of every tunic, cloth and jumper,
Each luncheon set and night dress case
That is embroidered in this place, –
And at a single glance must tell
If peasants use their cotton well,
Or else with indignation burn
Till stolen cotton they return;
Must know in their imagination
If green and mauve's a combination
That pleasing to the English minds;
Experiment until she finds
If beetroot, orange, purple, blue,
Will blend with pink of sickly hue;
(There's sackfuls waiting to be used,
That task will keep her well amused)
And try to use up all her stocks
In planning cushions, scarves and frocks;
Examine linen lengths and know,
When they've been made some years ago,
If they've been used, or just laid by,
And which of them are safe to buy.
Doubtless as these things you would expect

That one should do and not neglect
But there are many more beside: -
In a furmanka learn to ride
And not fall out and break one's bones
As it bumps over logs and stones;
Indulge in a continual fray
With frenzied landlords day by day;
Exterminate the rats and mice;
And give the peasants sound advice
How they can cure a nasty boil,
Supply them with cod liver oil,
Dress styes on eyelids, burns on legs;
To teach the cook to scramble eggs;
To lock up all that's in the house;
To tell the bed bug from a louse;
To add up column after column,
Banishing from one's mind a solemn
Dismal dark foreboding fear
Lest a deficit should appear;
(They do, you know, more oft than not
- A nasty little trick they've got)
To regulate the oats and hay
That both the horses eat each day;
Forbid the peasants at the door
To blow their noses on the floor;
(I hope you do not think it rude
To mention this; they're very crude ;)
Choose English books that will enthral
An English-speaking Russian-Pole;
If washing will remove a spot
Foretell, - or whether it will not.
Perhaps you'll say; "How can one know
In all these cases what to do?"

Or very possibly you guess
How one achieves a fair success!
The peasant's boils may flourish still;
The pigs and horses all be ill;
The stripes on rugs offend the eye;
And tunic hems hang all awry;
But no one's here to come along
And say "My dear, how very wrong!"
So one assume to one's delight
Whate'er one says and does is right!
And on these terms you will agree
Work's simple in the Industry!

Margaret Tregear, January 1925

On the Edge of the Pripyat Marshes

'Imagine a flat, flat marshy country, stretching for miles, and only broken here and there by the low line of woods; very bare, very bleak, very colourless. Villages of dark, wooden huts, mostly thatched, of one story, with a rough shelter of boughs and straw for the cow and a pig grunting round the doorway; wells with sides of logs, and a huge tree trunk balanced on a pole which swings back and pulls up the bucket. Roads ankle deep in mud, when there is no snow. And you will have a general idea of this part of Poland.

This part of Poland used to be more prosperous, before the people were driven away from here by the various armies that fought backward and forwards over the country – German and Russian, Austrian and Lithuanian. The people took what they could carry: a little of their finest linen, the ikon (their sacred picture), and other precious possessions, and they went to Russia. That was until the famine drove them back here again, and they arrived to find their land waste, their houses destroyed, and all their possessions gone, and they had to start life again… There were no houses, no brick and no wood, so whole families had to shelter in old dug-outs left in the trenches, or in lean-tos made of branches – all through a cold and snowy winter. There was no food, for the land had not been sown and there were no shops, and no money to buy anything with if there had been. They had to make bread out of grass and bits of bark from the trees, soup out of roots they pulled up, and of course many of them grew ill and died.'

This is the situation Margaret Tregear found when she stepped down from the train in rural eastern Poland in the fall of 1924 to join a relief project implemented by the Komitet Pomocy Polskim Kresom Wschodnim, (KPPKW – The Committee for Help to the Polish Eastern Borders). The KPPKW had been set up in 1924 to carry on work which was started in 1919 by British and American Quakers through the Society of Friends in Poland.

Horodec town. *As spring advanced, the un-paved streets of towns like Horodec became a sea of mud, churned by horse's hooves and wagon wheels. By summer they would return to dusty tracks. The simple log houses, mostly rebuilt since the war, belie the bustling economy which was re-emerging as peace settled in and the population returned to this district centre.*

The Quaker movement, which became known as the Society of Friends, began in 1652, during the English Civil War when new radical Protestant religious ideas sprang up in opposition to the limited reformation of the established English Church. The movement is characterised by four key theological ideas: the centrality of direct inward encounter with God and revelation; a consensus based approach to church decision making, which has also influenced decision making in non-church Quaker organisations; the spiritual equality of everyone, which included an early support for the involvement of women in all Quaker affairs; and a preference for pacifism rather than war, backed up by a commitment to relevant forms of social witness. In the early 20th century the commitment to pacifism and social witness inspired the Quakers or 'Friends' to become leaders in creating models of war relief work, reconstruction and conflict transformation.[7]

Having grown up in a well educated middle-class family in the small towns of southern England, Margaret was both fascinated and repelled by the conditions she encountered when she came to live in the war-ravaged town of Horodec. During World War One the Eastern Front had run directly through the districts of Horodec and Drohiczyn where she was to work for 11 months between October 1924 and August 1925. While the fighting had stopped, the country remained criss-crossed by collapsing trenches, acres of barbed wire, countless graveyards and fields of unburied bones. Among this devastation, recently returned refugees were struggling to re-establish their lives. The Friends hoped their work would make the refugees' difficult lives a little bit easier.

Between the fall of 1924 and July 1925 Margaret wrote a personal journal in the form of a set of candid letters about her experiences. The letters were circulated among a group of her women friends who were dispersed across Europe and as far away as India, and finally returned to Margaret. Thirteen of this series of letters are now deposited in the Library of the Religious Society of Friends in London. Margaret's letters provide a window into the inner workings of an early international development project, and show how the different actors involved – international staff, local staff, project beneficiaries, and various local power-brokers – struggled to reach their different objectives. The people involved with the project had many different motivations and expectations – all of which were often difficult to understand for the short-term international aid workers like Margaret.

Margaret's story takes place in a historical period when new international aid agencies were expanding rapidly and providing humanitarian aid on a whole new scale in response to the refugee crises of World War One. The story told in these old letters may help us to understand some of the challenges still faced by people working in humanitarian aid today. At the same time the letters provide a compelling and surprisingly timeless account of the ups and downs of the enthusiastic international volunteer as she tries to make sense of how projects really work in a multicultural environment.

Where the canal meets the railroad

Margaret was assigned to a Friends' project based in the small town of Horodec. Horodec is located between Kobryn and Pinsk on the Polesia railway, directly east of Brest in the province of Polesia. Polesia is now part of the post-Soviet Republic of Belarus, but in 1924 after six years of war, it had finally been ceded from the Russian empire to the newly constituted country of Poland.

The province of Polesia is a featureless flat region and at the centre, surrounding the Bug and Pripyat rivers, is 6,500 square miles of the Pripyat Marshes. Up to the 1880s the only reliable way to cross the region was by water. Significant transit only began with the building of the 75km long Dnieper-Bug Canal in 1784. The canal crossed the watershed between the Dnieper River and the Bug River and made river trade possible all the way from the Black Sea to the Baltic Sea port of Danzig. This canal was extended as far as Horodec in 1841, turning the small town into a centre of trade.

In 1884 the new Brest-Pinsk Polesia railway bridged the Dnieper-Bug Canal near Horodec and a train station was built for the town. As a centre of increasing importance Horodec also had a post office. In 1910 a 'highway' was built between Horodec and the next market town of Antopol five miles away, and the main streets of the town were paved. However, there were no significant regional roads in Polesia before the 1920s and only 88 miles were added up until 1936. Horodec did not have a telephone before 1928, although there was a telegraph attached to the railway. Before World War One Horodec was a bustling little trading town with a population of about 2,500. [1, 2]

In the late 1940s Jewish immigrants to America who had grown up in Horodec, and left Poland before World War Two and the Holocaust, recorded their memories of Horodec before World War One in a Yizkor book.

'This shtetl, which was encircled by fields and gardens, was divided into two unequal parts by the Dnieper-Bug canal and by two smaller canals called Free-canals on both sides. A large and high wooden bridge with smaller bridges on both sides of the river joined the two parts of the shtetl. The railroad line operated in the south side of the shtetl, not more than 300 meters from the houses. The residents would always know the time, from morning till night, according to the passenger trains which passed by the shtetl four times a day. The whistles of the locomotives were always a welcome noise and the trains with the colored wagons an unending source of interest. The train would cross the river over an iron bridge that was painted a deep green and would park about a mile from the shtetl, near the station which was named after the river, Dnieper-Bug.

The river, with its two bridges and the railroad line with station gave the shtetl a certain prestige and an excuse to feel superior to the neighboring towns. Workers in Antopol, for example, which was much larger, would need to travel to Horodets. Antopoler coachmen would have to bring their passengers to the Horodets train station, which was quite far to go...

Large and small lumber and wood merchants from all over Russia would stop over in Horodets for a few days on their way to the port of Danzig (today's Gdansk), during which time the lumber would swim in the Horodets canal. In the winter the peasants would bring the lumber to the river's edge. In the spring would start the feverish activity of assembling the barges from which Jews and gentiles alike made their living. During the entire summer barges would be pulled along the river carrying various people from Russia and also from other foreign countries...

Along the two riverside parks which lined the river's edge, had grown a forest of beautiful trees. There, the youth of the town enjoyed themselves. In summer they would sail off on a raft or they could bathe in the clean, clear water of the canal...

But the river was the overriding reminder that the town was split into two unequal parts, "The Street" and "The Market", The "Street", that is, the Jewish street, extended for a distance of four to five blocks from Old Man Saul's tavern to Gedalya Yudel's shop. Beyond this shop began the Gentile street, or, as we called it, Kobrinner street (since it led to the county seat in Kobrin). .... The street was a long one. From one side it went toward Kobrin and from the other side it went toward the village Makhvedevitsh....

The greater part of the town was called the "Market". In the Market were located the Jewish houses as well as the shops, which were larger and finer and spaced over a larger area than those located on the "Street". The "Market" didn't have any pipe shops as, for example, were on Kobrin street. The shops in Horodets stood in an empty place, nearly four blocks in area, on which grew grass in the summer and was quite muddy in the winter. The houses on both sides of the "Market" were quite nice and large and were inhabited by several rich home owners. There, also would be found the Russian Greek Orthodox church and the Polish Roman Catholic Church. On the eastern side, opposite the Market, on the way to Antopol, not far from the Post Office, stood the Pravaslann monastery. It had a stone parking lot next to a great meadow which belonged to the priest. The walls were painted white and the roof with its cupolas were painted either blue or green…

Opposite the Market, on the southern side, stood the government public school. There, a few hundred peasant children of various parents went to study during the three to four winter months of the year. One individual teacher would teach all these children reading, writing and arithmetic at the same time, in one great room. The children would sit, crowded together on long benches. The little that they learned in the short winter session would be completely forgotten during the remaining months of the year when they would have to work with their parents in the field.

Next to the school stood the "Pazsharne" (militia) command and the police station from Volast, which had its own lockup for people who were arrested and needed to be held overnight or longer and then transported with other convicts to various parts of the country.

The Catholic Church stood in a side alley of the Market which we called the Landowner's street. It was an old, high wooden building, unpainted and overgrown with weeds which gave the impression of neglect. In truth, at one time these neglected buildings belonged to the Russian Orthodox church and those which remained on the Market used to be Polish. But, after the Pavskanye (Polish insurrection) [1863-1864], the Poles were removed and the Russians took over for themselves the nicer buildings. On this Landowner's street lived Shakhnav the Uriadnik (police constable), the Diak and a few Polish gentiles. At the time of the First World War there were hardly any Poles in Horodets. We could count them on our fingers, they were so few.'[1]

Divided by religion, united in trade

The trade which developed in Horodec at the confluence of the railway and canal included grain, whisky, hogs, candles, ceramics and timber. In 1860, before the railway reached Horodec, 92 ships and barges were unloaded at Horodec while 41 were loaded for export. After the railway came, that trade increased. While Horodec was a small rural town there was a variety of small traders and craftsmen working in the community, including shoemakers, tailors, dressmakers, felt makers, bookbinders, carpenters, drillers, blacksmiths, butchers, bakers, taverns, wagon drivers, sawyers and bricklayers. Trade in fish caught in the canal was another local business. [1] A significant local business was the timber trade, with logs being shipped down the canal from the area in large rafts as far as Germany or Danzig. Local experience with the lumber trade may explain why the Friends chose to locate one of their outposts here when their primary project work was helping returned refugees fetch timber from government forests to rebuild their houses. One of the Friends' landlords, Mr Vinograd, was in the timber trade.

The local economy was structured along ethnic lines. On the first day of each month in the Russian calendar, there was a fair or market in the central square of Horodec. The Belorussian peasant farmers, all Orthodox Christians, from the smaller surrounding villages would bring their livestock and farm products to the monthly market. The peasants were mainly subsistence farmers but they also sold some surplus agricultural products like calves, horses, hens, eggs, potatoes, corn, oats, millet, barley, oil seeds, mushrooms, pig hair, sheep wool and home-made flax linen. They sold these products to Jewish traders in the town who then supplied the peasants with a range of household items like sewing thread, fabric for clothing, herring, heating oil, candles, mushrooms, salt, fish oil for their boots and tar for their wagon wheels, and ironware such as scythes, sickles, ploughs and other implements. Although the peasants made many of their own clothes, some also bought services from skilled Jewish craftsmen like tailors and shoemakers, and they needed the blacksmiths to repair their tools. However, the peasants did not hire

Antopol Market. *Small towns like Horodec, and nearby Antopol, had busy monthly markets where the Belorussian peasants came to trade agricultural products for manufactured goods with local Jewish businessmen.*

Jewish craftsmen for the building trades as they tended to be well-skilled themselves in building homes and barns. The Jewish building craftsmen mostly worked for the large estate owners who were Russian, and later Polish. Jewish farmers, who were not allowed to own land under the Tsar's decree of 1864, often leased milk production and orchards on the large estates and managed agricultural production for the landlords. [3]

Torn apart by war and evacuation

In 1924, Horodec was part of the Polish province of Polesia, but before World War One the town had been under the Russian Empire. During World War One the area was occupied by a German army under Von Linsingen from September 1915 though November 1918. After March 1918 when the Germans signed the Treaty of Brest-Litovsk with the new Bolshevik government of Russia, the area was briefly under Ukrainian administration until the new Polish government took control in March 1919. During the subsequent Polish-Bolshevik War of 1919–20 Horodec was on the front line and changed hands eight times in ten days. When the March 1921 Treaty of Riga ended this war, the province was ceded to Poland. During the six years of war most of the villages in the area suffered serious damage and disruption, and the population of the area was considerably reduced by evacuations, epidemics and war casualties. [3-5]

The Belarusian peasants probably suffered the worst losses. Between mid-August and the end of September 1915 the Tsarist forces retreated rapidly under attack by the German Army of the Bug, and evacuated the Belarusian peasants with them. With almost no notice, most peasants were forced to abandon their homes and crops and leave with few possessions or food. Following a 'scorched earth' policy, the Russian army set fire to the peasant villages and towns as they left. The peasants were pushed onwards to the railway stations where they were loaded into box cars and sent east across Russia. Contemporary estimates suggest that as many as 3,300,000 Poles, Jews, Ruthenians, Belarusians and Ukrainians were deported from eastern Poland into Russia in 1915 and 1916. A significant number ended up in the Samara province east of the Urals. [5, 6]

The Quakers initiate relief work in Russia

In 1916 the English Friends, recently experienced with refugee relief on the Western Front in France, sent representatives into Russia to find out how they might help the refugees displaced by the war on the Eastern Front. When it was clear that the Russian province with the greatest density of refugees was Samara, they negotiated to set up a refugee assistance programme which was run from the provincial capital of Buzuluk. Between July 1916 and 1919 they provided relief for refugees, including medical services, food and clothing distributions, work programmes and they also set up an orphanage. It was while implementing work programmes for refugees in Buzuluk that the Friends first tested the idea of helping women and girls earn money from their traditional crafts of spinning, weaving and embroidery. One of the English Friends who helped establish the work in Buzuluk was Florence Barrow. Florence ran a district relief programme for a few months and then went on to manage the Friends' orphanage and its workroom for 13 months in 1917–18. [8]

When the Friends closed down their programme in Buzuluk in October 1918, in the face of increasing danger created by the Civil War, some refugees from Samara were already moving back to Poland to escape the war and rapidly developing famine. The refugees started out on a long and treacherous journey towards the west while the Friends travelled east around the world back to the US and England. Eventually some of them would meet again in the eastern Provinces of Poland when the Friends began a programme to assist returning refugees in 1919.

The Quakers follow the crisis back to Poland

The first team of American and English Friends began working in Poland in 1919 while fighting between Poland and the Bolsheviks was still going on. At the time there were estimates that up to five million people were at the point of starvation in the eastern provinces of the new Poland [9]. Typhus, and the lice which carried it, travelled with returning refugees across this war zone and back into Poland, igniting a major epidemic there in 1919. The Friends' first project brought in a team of 25 volunteers to undertake the dangerous work of fighting typhus by setting up facilities to delouse returning refugees and their belongings.

The Friends began their Polish work as a very small player among international relief agencies in Poland. The biggest relief agency, the American Relief Administration (ARA), started in 1919 to implement a vast humanitarian programme which at its peak fed 1,300,000 hungry Polish children daily through 7,290 community kitchens, and also provided clothing. ARA worked through 14 regional offices, 198 district offices and had 620 paid employees and 2,000 volunteers. [10] The Friends helped implement a small part of this program, feeding 1,650 children with ARA food in 1919–20. [11] Other much larger partners of the ARA included the American Red Cross (ARC) and the American Jewish Joint Distribution Committee (JDC) and the YMCA and the YWCA. In 1919, before the disruptions of the Polish-Soviet war, Horodec and Drohiczyn were two of the villages where the JCD was distributing ARA relief through soup-kitchens for children and clothing distributions. While the big American agencies dominated the field of relief in Poland, other international organizations were active during this period including the International Committee of the Red Cross, the British Red Cross, Save the Children Fund and the Union Internationale de Secours aux Enfants. [12] The ARA and the ARC closed their activities in Poland in 1922, and most other international agencies were asked to leave by 1924. The Quakers relied on carefully cultivated connections to continue working until 1929 when the Polish government closed down all remaining international aid projects.

As the typhus epidemic subsided in 1920–21, the Friends moved on to helping refugees re-establish farms by providing tractors, horses, implements and seeds. [11] In 1921 they set up the Cotton Seed Meal Project, to make use of a donation from the ARA of hundreds of tons of cotton seed meal. The Friends' plan was to use this meal indirectly to improve the nutrition of hungry children. The cotton seed meal was given to local farmers to feed to their milk cows. The farmers would then contribute their surplus milk to orphanages and children's homes.

By the middle of 1921 however, the Friends realised that there were pressing needs in the eastern border areas of Poland to which they wanted to respond. When the Treaty of Riga ended the Polish-Soviet war in 1921, up to 1,500,000 of the 3,300,000 refugees who had left for Russia six years earlier travelled back into what was now independent Poland. About 600,000 of these travelled independently, while 900,000 were returned by the Soviet government. The evacuations arranged by the Soviet government were not well organised, and in many groups up to half those travelling died of hunger, disease and/or cold in transit, either in the trains, or waiting in transit camps along the way. Rail journeys for some involved six weeks to three months crowded 25 to 30 people together in a boxcar with little food and no sanitary facilities. Others made an even slower journey on foot or in wagons. The new state of Poland was ill-prepared for the deluge of impoverished, diseased, and homeless people. At its peak, the flow of 20,000 people a week overwhelmed the border reception facilities. [6] Representatives from the Friends' Warsaw Mission visited their small outpost at Drohiczyn and witnessed throngs of recently returned refugees in 1921. [13]

In 1920 another group of Friends had returned to Soviet Russia to help distribute food to orphanages in and around Moscow and in 1921 they returned to their old stomping ground of Buzuluk, which was now at the centre of a region where a famine of unprecedented proportions had broken out. The remaining refugees in the famine zone were now desperate to leave and make their way home. In Russia and in Poland, the Friends worked to reduce the appalling death rates at either end of this stream of refugees. Florence Barrow, who knew some of these refugees personally from her time in Russia, took over the leadership of the Friends' Polish unit and led the efforts to support the greatly reduced number of refugees who made it home to their villages in eastern Poland.

The refugees come home to no homes

'What did they return to? Certainly not to the land and buildings they had left; but to a waste of battle-torn trenches, land covered with endless reaches of barbed wire, and filled with shells waiting to explode and kill the peasant who sets his spade into the soil to prepare for his first crop. Forests of birch whose roots will defy eradication for the next ten years cover the fields that were once waving with grain. It is impossible adequately to describe the wilderness left on a modern battle front. It took 6,000,000 men working for three years with the most efficient machines science could invent to make that land what it is today; now a few thousand peasants, starved, half-naked, return and with their bare hands try to recover from it their lost homes.'[11]

Almost the only things brought back by the refugees were diseases and the seeds of diseases.[14]

The homeless refugees moved in to dugout shelters in the trenches left behind by the retreating armies, and improvised shacks. Margaret wrote:

'You'd probably like to know what their houses are like inside. I've only been into two or three – but they were of very different kinds. I've seen an awful dug-out about six feet square where an old man lives, a kind of lean-to build of moss, and branches where there is a family, and the peasant house where we have the loom room is pretty bad. As you go in the door there is more of a stable than a room, beaten earth for the floor, a pig's trough and hay piled up in the corner. The woman and her two sons all live in the next room, dirty, with only a small table and stool for furniture and some boards near the stove for a bed...

In other houses, however, I have seen...two rooms: one with a mud floor which serves as a stable barn and pig sty in the winter, but which is now beautifully swept; the other with [floor] boards, unless the family is very poor, and perhaps has a wicker cradle hanging from the ceiling, and a big square monument of white plaster which looks rather like a family vault, but which is really the stove. The sides are of thick cement so that the heat comes through gently and it is on top of that that all the

Living in a dugout. *A homeless refugee improvises a new home from a soldier's 'dug out' left behind by the Germans after the trench warfare on the Eastern Front between 1915 and 1918. Dugouts were cramped, damp and at risk of flooding. An early Friends' project provided timber to rebuild proper houses.*

Inside a peasant house. *A home-made basket-work cradle hanging from the ceiling holds the youngest child in a simple peasant home. In the absence of a cash income, everything the peasants had was made with their own hands. The project aimed to give women enough cash to buy manufactured necessities like soap, medicines and paraffin.*

members of the family (or as many as can) make their beds. The others lie on these boards near, running round the side of the room. There is a small table, a broom of twigs, and a pail or two in the corner, but no other furniture unless, it is winter, the loom is up. The somewhat gaudy picture of the Virgin with the festoons of pink paper round it is the family ikons.

It was a terrible struggle starting life again, but their piece of land was here, and how should they live elsewhere! The first harvest was the beginning. They ground their corn between the huge stones of the village windmill, kept what they needed for their year's bread and bartered the rest for things that they needed. Potatoes too, they had planted and flax for their linen, and the Government and the Missions helped them to get a cow, a pig, hens or a horse as the case might be.'

By 1924 the situation of the returned refugees had stabilised somewhat and the Friends began to wrap up their 'relief' activities and move into what would today be termed 'development'. Margaret described the life of the peasants she met in some detail:

'At first there were few animals in the villages, but now most families have their pig, some hens and a great many have a cow or sheep or a horse as well. One of the children of the village drives the whole number out onto the marshes and guards them from straying either into the corn or into the bog. It is quaint to see them all running down the village street as they are driven back at night, each cow or sheep turning of its own accord into its own gateway.

On either side of a long village street are low brown wooden thatched houses; and above each house towers a tall tree. At the end of most of the roofs there is a stork's nest as large as a wash tub and it needs to be, for the babies are so nearly as large [as] their parents now that it is difficult to tell which is which. The mud yard is neatly swept, and over the wooden palings are spread lengths of new linen, or newly made shirts, and stuck upside down to dry are the shapely black pots in which the peasant set their sour milk. That is if it is a week day - if it is Sunday the family itself will be ornamenting the palings, not stuck upside down on top, but squatting round on the ground outside, unless they are lucky enough to

Wattle house. *In the absence of help to collect and mill timber from the government forests, returned refugees used ancient materials like wattle to make basic accommodation.*

have a fallen tree stump for a seat. And very splendid they look in their Sunday best. The women with red embroidered sleeves to their blouses, and their aprons embroidered to match, over red striped skirts and the whitest of head handkerchiefs tied under their chins. The little girls, even those of four and five, in the villages, are dressed in just the same quaint old fashioned way, and the boys in their white grey home spun coats and long trousers, and straw hats are small editions of the men.

Most of them talk what is called White Russian and only understand their own funny dialect. Of course most of them can't read or write; there were no schools in the Eastern country districts, and the whole of their life is very primitive and on a low level. It is like going back two or three centuries. Each family aims more or less at supplying its own need. They all have their piece of land (tho the soil round here is very poor), they grow rye for bread, and potatoes; flax which they spin and weave for clothes and their sheep give them wool and sheepskins. Some keep cows too and most people have hens and pigs, but they don't often eat meat or eggs.

The peasants live on their rye bread, soup and potatoes all the year round, with sometimes eggs or sour milk, and on great occasions sausage from the pig! But as a rule they sell their meat, eggs and poultry to the towns. In the summer there are fresh vegetables for variety, bilberries and wild raspberries to be picked, and morella cherries that they grow in their gardens. The summer is a great time for them. Harvest is the most important and the most joyous time of the year for them. Everyone except cripples, babies and helpless old people works in the fields. The houses are shut up. Babies are taken along and hung in a cradle from a tripod of sticks and covered with an apron from the glare of the sun. If you pass people reaping they will stop and bind a swathe of corn around you giving you all the good wishes for health and luck in the coming year.

There is a long long winter to come when no work outside is possible. The marshes are frozen and covered with snow more often than not, the entire season. In the autumn firewood is hauled in and the women turn their attention to clothing. Their land and their animals furnish them

Above and opposite: Sheepskin coats. *The Belarusian peasants made most of their clothes from their own sheepskins and hand woven wool and linen. The Friend's project built on the women's traditional skills with loom and needles.*

with that [?] flax and wool are spun and woven. It is thrilling to see the women with just the same sort of spinning wheel that you associate with the wicked fairy in the Sleeping Beauty. The wool is woven very thickly and then shrunk to produce a kind of light-coloured felt which they join in wonderful fashions with bits of red leather for ornament to make coats for the men and women.

A man will often have a coat made of sheepskin as well (or instead) and certainly a round hat with the woolly part of the sheepskin outside. The flax makes linen for shirts, blouses, aprons and undergarments of every description; as a rule the material is fairly coarse, but each woman has one or two really fine lengths of which she is justly proud. They make sandals of reeds for the winter but go barefoot in the summer. It is a kind of Robinson Crusoe existence, where they grow or make nearly everything they need. The things they have to buy are salt, paraffin, and head handkerchiefs. Why they buy head handkerchiefs instead of making them I don't know but they do. And they seem to use a great many. However dirty anything else may be, a peasant women always has a clean head handkerchief and she keeps everything she possesses wrapped up in her third, fourth and fifth best.

Perhaps, later on, they will have more possessions in their house, but they are only just beginning to get straight again since they came back from Russia. When the war began they fled with all the other peasants to Russia where they stayed until the Bolshevik wars were over, and when in 1920 or 1921 they began to come back, they found everything destroyed. In some villages only the stump of a tree was left to show where the village had been – in others only the houses had been burnt. So they built a dugout and covered it with branches, or made a hut of straw and boughs, or a half underground dwelling built of turf and huddled together there for the winter, living, those of them who survived on bits of bark, roots and grass, and fish from the marshes unless they could get rations from one of the relief missions who came to help. In time however

Shelter first. *Erling Kjekstad supervising local workers in Horodec running the Friends' saw mill. From 1922 to 1924 a Friends' project helped cut, haul and mill timber to rebuild almost 2,000 refugees' houses.*

the Government and the Friends Relief Mission helped to provide wood for houses, flax seed and rye seed for sowing, cows, pigs and horses, and bit by bit they began to rebuild their old life.'

This was the situation of the peasant population which Margaret hoped to help improve through the Quaker project she had joined.

A Project for the Women and Girls

The Quaker organisation in Poland

The Friends' work in Poland began as a joint effort of the Friends' War Victims Relief Committee (FRC) based in London, and American Friends Service Committee (AFSC) based in Philadelphia. During an exploratory mission two senior English Friends and one American contacted the new Polish government and negotiated an initial relief mandate to fight the typhus epidemic.

English Friends had a history of organizing relief to refugees long before World War One. Friends were active with famine relief in Ireland in 1847–48 during the potato famine and worked in Finland after the Crimean War. The first formal relief committee set up by the British Friends delivered aid to French peasants during the Franco-Prussian War in 1870. The Friends organised again to provide relief in Eastern Europe in 1876, in South Africa during the Boer War in 1900, in the Balkans in 1912, and between 1914 and 1923 in France. From 1914 to 1923 English contributions to the Friends international relief activities were managed by the Friends War Victims Relief Committee (FRC). Responsibility for the English support for the Friends' work in Poland was transferred from the FRC to the Friends' Council for International Service (CIS) in November 1923. [15]

The American Friends Service Committee (AFSC) was established in 1917 after the Americans entered World War One to provide American Friends and other conscientious objectors with an alternative to military service during the war. AFSC first sent volunteers to work alongside British Friends with refugees in France in 1917. In 1919 AFSC was asked by the American Relief Administration (ARA) to implement a massive relief programme in post-war Germany which fed up to one million children a day with American food aid.[16]

The Friends' Relief Mission Unit was set up in Poland in 1919, with headquarters in Warsaw. The Mission was jointly supported and

A symbol of peace. *Volunteers working with the Friends wore this badge.*

managed by the FRC and AFSC. A separate Industries Committee was set up in 1923 to manage the women's embroidery project which had grown from a small initiative in 1921. The Industries Committee brought the Friends together with representatives of Polish Women's organisations under the chairmanship of a Polish woman, Mrs. Czarlinska. An English Quaker, Jane Pontefract, was responsible for general management of the industry.

In 1924 a joint English-American-Polish Advisory Committee was established to begin the process of localising the management of the remaining activities. The Komitet Pomocy Polskim Kresom Wschodnim,

(KPPKW) or Committee for Help to the Polish Eastern Borders was active from 1924 through 1929, although the Friends in England and America continued to provide help with fundraising and recruiting international volunteers. The old Industries Committee became a sub-committee of the new KPPKW. In 1925 the KPPKW's main activities were the Women's Industries and the Kolpin Agricultural School and Orphanage at Stradecz.[14, 17]

A mission outpost in Horodec

At their peak of activity in Poland, the Friends Mission maintained five outposts. Most of these outposts were closed in 1924 when the programme to provide timber to rebuild refugee's houses came to an end. The Friends Mission Outpost at Horodec was one of the early outposts established by the mission and it continued to be a base for the Women's Industries after the other programmes and outposts of the Mission were closed. Margaret wrote,

We are miles from a post office, two from a station, no shops (or practically none, though one of or two of the houses call themselves stores and you can buy flour and sugar and a few such things) – no [electric] lighting, of course, but lamps and candles, and undrinkable water. And yet, I am always being reminded, this is a town and not a village!! There are about three streets and a green, but we do possess a police office and a school.

Our quarters are rather superior. We have part of two different houses, and though our furniture is largely made out of packing cases, we have covers for most things and manage to make them look quite nice. I have got so used to them now that it is difficult to tell you just what they look like.

The Friends rented parts of two large log houses, and a barn between them. Several rooms were rented in the house of the Catholic priest, who lived in the rest of the house. The sleeping quarters for the women were in this house along with a kitchen and dining room. Office and work space was rented in a second house which belonged to a Jewish merchant,

Mission outpost, Horodec, 1925. *One of the two houses rented by the Mission. One belonged to the local Catholic Priest and the other to a local Jewish business man. In a complicated arrangement, the Friends rented part of each house, plus stables and out buildings, to put together enough space to run their project. Their use of so much space was a concern for the local population, facing a serious post-war shortage of housing.*

Haim-Nisl Vinograd who also lived in the rest of this house with his family. Both houses were heated with thick brick stoves, three to six feet across at the base, and extending up to the ceiling which were built into interior walls and when stoked radiated heat into two or three rooms. But fuel shortages left the houses cool in winter, and the Friends staff all wore heavy clothes inside. Water was fetched from a dug well in the yard and was raised by a bucket on the end of a long levered pole, and needed boiling to be drinkable. There was no bathroom, but a zinc wash tub could be used to bath in. Henry Hamilton described the Vinograd's house,

'The house was built of logs. It was new, the walls and corners were straight and square and papered with what looked like a good quality wrapping paper painted a robin's-egg blue. They were clean, and the wide pine boards of the floor showed signs of recent scrubbing. The room into which the front door opened was perhaps fourteen by sixteen feet square. Five doors lead to the other rooms at the back and sides, indicating that the house was quite large. Case of papers, books, and other equipment stood against the walls; two long tables under the windows served as desks. This was the outpost office.' [4]

These were some of the best houses in the town, but conditions still seemed very 'rural' to Margaret.

When I first came it was still warm and flies were swarming everywhere, all over everything, especially the food. Even now lady-birds, mosquitoes, beetles, flies, spiders and heaps of strange and unknown insects inhabit the rooms, and occasionally bugs make their appearance... Another thing that I had to put up with when I first came was mice. All over the place! On the floor, on the bookshelves, on the stoves and in the walls. They particularly like the paste that the windows were pasted up with and would swing up on the curtains and nibble while you wrote at the table below, with the utmost unconcern. What unnerved me most was when they did that on the windows above my bed and slithered

Hand dug well. *The peasants in this log house raised their water with a bucket on a long pole pivoted beside the wooden walled well. Getting water this way for laundry in the winter might seem like difficult living conditions, but this picture shows a big improvement on the post-war conditions.*

down the wall in the middle of the night, and with all possible speed I procured a cat. Since then we've reduced the number in this house to about one and in the other the only place they still attack is the food cupboard where we catch about three a week.

Generating income through embroidery

The Friends' experience led them to conclude that '[t]o be idly happy and a refugee is a contradiction in terms',[14] and so they consistently tried to include some practical activities as part of their support to refugees. Such activities were designed to help normalize the refugees' situation, both by providing some income and regaining self-confidence through helping themselves. The embroidery project, known among the Friends in Poland as the 'Women's Industries', grew out of the experience of the Friends in Russia in 1917–18 and also in the Carpathians in 1920–21, where women and girl refugees were paid to engage in their traditional crafts of spinning, weaving and embroidery. The products were sold, either locally in the case of woollen cloth, or in England in the case of embroidered articles. Profits were ploughed back into the project.

By 1924 the embroidery industry was well developed and that year almost 5,000 women produced 18,000 embroidered products for the English market, valued at £3,129 (roughly $190,000 in 2010 US dollars).[17] The project staff bought local linen and cut it into appropriate pieces for a range of items like tea towels, tea cosies, tray cloths, etc. High quality embroidery cotton was brought in from England. The linen and an appropriate amount of embroidery cotton were handed out to women at 'distributions' and 'wages' were paid when they returned the embroidered item. Margaret explained how the project worked to her friends.

'One way of helping that the Friends found was to give [the women] embroidery to do, like [the embroidery] most of them had worked on their aprons or on the collars and fronts of the men's best shirts, pay them wages for that, and then sell the embroideries in England and America.

And of course that is what I am here to look after. Flax is grown in the fields – the women soak it, beat it, spin and wind the threads and then weave it into linen in their homes for their clothes and for any linen that is needed about the house. Any they have over we buy – more than a hundred metres every week, and have it cut up into almost every kind of article you can think of ready to be embroidered. We have one day a week for this district [Horodec] and one for the Drohiczyn district, when we distribute the work and the cotton and take back the finished work and pay wages.

The women get up at daylight and start from their homes regardless of the time (they have no clocks or watches!) so that there is often quite a small crowd waiting outside before I'm even out of bed. We give them numbers to that each gets her proper turn and they can go away and wait in the village if they like until it comes. Sometimes they crowd in regardless of the numbers and refuse to stir – and then we have to treat them like naughty children, give them three minutes to get out and then anyone who is left in the room at the end of time gets no work or pay. But

A distribution. *Women wait in front of a log building to return embroidered items, collect their pay, and pick up materials for their next embroidery project. And while they wait – often long hours – they embroider. They all cover their heads, but have bare feet.*

Turning spare moments into money. *The project worked from the premise that the peasant women had 'spare time' which they could put towards income generation, if they had the right resources.*

generally they are very patient and because they all will come early in the morning some have to wait nearly all day.

They are very warmly dressed no matter how patched and dirty, generally in thick homespun coats and skirts, or coats made of sheepskins sewn together and turned inside out. They wear shawls round their heads and some times one over their shoulders as well; aprons; and often a kind of sandal made out of felt and reeds. Their bundles of embroideries plus the black rye bread they bring for their meal is done up in a handkerchief which is used for every purpose under the sun, and fastened up in their apron, bang in front of their middles, which gives a very quaint figure. Often inside the outside one is a second in which the work is tied up securely – her number card will be in a third, the remaining cotton in a fourth.

As a side-line to embroideries we run weavings as well as embroideries, but whereas over a thousand women take embroidery during the year, we only have about ten loom workers. We have two rooms in the village, one with four and the other with three looms, and have just set another up in the entrance to this house. The girls weave rugs and bags, cushion covers, runners, bedspreads, scarves, etc. It's most interesting work to watch and to organize. I only wish I could send you specimens of all the kinds of things that are made here. It would be so much more interesting.

Some of the workers are quite little girls, from nine upwards, and they do very nice work – mostly while they are minding cattle in the fields. One looked so wee the other day that I asked her how old she was; she just threw back her head and laughed and said "Goodness me! Who could possibly know a thing like that?" But what is funnier than their not know their ages is that most of them don't even know their surnames. We have only got them right this year because each worker has to bring a certificate from the head man of the village, but if you ask the women themselves they suggest their neighbour's name, or a cousin's and generally only manage to tell you the right one after much consultation with all the other women in the room.

It would take too long to tell you all about them, and how funny they are at distributions, just like big and rather naughty children. ... When

Embroidering on the go. *This is obviously a posed picture, but some women did take their embroidery around with them so they could quickly turn around the work in-time for the next distribution.*

they come in they give me a card with their name and number. I look up the record of their work. They can do beautiful work, but often try to skimp and give narrow patterns, too little hemstitching and so on to try and keep the cotton that is over. When you get a really good piece of work you have to be careful not to praise it too much, because even if you pay extra for it, the women will go away grumbling that you haven't given her enough. That is rather a pity, I think. Quite one in three tries to steal cotton and we have some dreadful and some very amusing scenes – as we don't pay them or give them more work till they return it. They begin always by denying most indignantly and swearing (really swearing) that they haven't got it. Then some get angry and threaten to got to the police, other are pathetic and weep and tell us all their misfortune; but nearly all turn up with the cotton next time. They have all sorts of excuses – "My mother didn't give it to me", "My sister gave it away" – or they say "This isn't what you gave me. I bought it." In spite of this, and they are too ignorant to know better, they are really very likeable people, and have a great sense of humour, and sometimes they are so stupid that they are unconsciously funny. They do beautiful work though, and need the money that they get for it very badly.'

Margaret's responsibilities included taking kit bags of finished embroidered products on the train to Warsaw, and returning to Horodec with more embroidery cotton and enough cash to pay the women for their work at the next round of 'distributions'.

'The trains are very poor and the people travelling generally very dirty. The carriages are frightfully overheated and smelly and are lit by candles at night. As there are practically no corridor carriages the man who looks after the candles, the conductor and the ticket collector, etc. walk along the footboards and pop in at one door and out of the other while the train is going. Also nearly all the travelling is done by night which seems strange and inconvenient when you first arrive, but like everything else one soon gets used to it.'

The necessity of carrying large amounts of cash for the project worried her constantly and her letters mention her fear of train robberies several times. During Margaret's time the currency had been temporarily stabilised, but in the previous four years the country had suffered from hyperinflation as the government printed money to cover regular budget deficits. Calculating fair wages for the women embroiderers was an ongoing problem. At one point wages were based on the value of rye flour, but the value of this commodity also fluctuated with the seasonal harvests, so after 1923 wages were tied to the price of paraffin and soap. At the peak period of inflation the money required to pay out women in smaller denominations added up to many millions in the deflated currency and filled a small suitcase. [4,17,18]

'Lots of unemployed people in these districts have turned into bandits and go round making raids in different places. They send a polite notice to the estate owner or priest or whoever they are going to rob, turn up and have supper with him, and after elegant and amicable conversation politely request him to hand over all his money and valuables – which he generally seems to do. There have been so many attacks on trains that armed police ride on all the engines and in every coach of the train. My fellow worker from Warsaw had her rucksack stolen just after Xmas, from the rack over her head – and the man would have made off with her fur coat too, if she hadn't kept tight hold and given chase. So you can imagine, it's a fairly exciting business bringing back £50 - £100 [£2,000-5000 or $3,000-6,000 in 2010 currency] from Warsaw. And you never know who may be in league with them - the man at the station buffet in Drohiczyn where we go for our other distribution, was convicted not long ago, so we cling tightly to our wages money as we travel backwards and forwards.'

When Margaret headed out to visit the villages where the women workers lived, there were no trains or even roads.

'Nearly all the travelling, except for long distances, is done in a wonderful kind of wagon called a furmanka. It has no springs, and you sit on top of a bundle of hay and get tossed into the air, jerked forwards and backwards and sideways, rattle everything you have inside up and down to such an extent that you feel quite certain it will never straighten out again, and come to the end of your journey utterly astonished that you are

Local transport. *To reach small communities off the railroad, project staff hired a furmanka. These wagons had no suspension, and the only comfort offered passengers was a pile of straw as they bounced along the rough tracks that passed for local roads. Sometimes passengers were bounced right out of the wagon!*

still in the furmanka. It is said that one quite often gets thrown out, but I am still waiting for that experience. Between here and the post town there is a road – what we should call a bad road but an excellent road for Poland – but in every other direction there are only tracks, and you are always bumping in and out of holes, over logs and bits of boulder. Generally in the winter you have a much better time than we have had because when there is a lot of snow, everyone drives in sleighs. But though we have had snow at intervals it has never really been deep enough. However, I did drive in a sleigh once so I feel that I haven't quite missed the experience.'

The embroidered products produced in these remote communities ended up far from the villages where they were made, in the homes of supportive families in England and America. Margaret explained to her friends how they could help with the sales program.

'If any of you are interested in seeing some of their work and are in London go to Devonshire House, 136 Bishopsgate, London, E.C. Miss Jordan

THE FRIENDS' COUNCIL *for*
INTERNATIONAL SERVICE

*invites you and your friends
to a Sale of*

Polish Peasant Handicrafts

to be held

at SUCKLING HALL, NORWICH

On Friday and Saturday, December 9 and 10

From 11 a.m. to 6.30 p.m.

The Exhibition will be opened at 12 noon on Friday, December 9th
by Miss Colman

EMBROIDERIES ON HAND-MADE LINEN &
HANDWOVEN DRESS LENGTHS, ETC.
THE WORK OF PEASANT
WOMEN AND GIRLS IN
EASTERN POLAND

Fund raising sales. Many 'Polish' embroideries were sold at events like this in England and America in the 1920s and 1930s. Profits were circulated back through the 'industry' to generate wages for the Belarusian peasant women and cover administrative costs of the English and American committees (Original in the Library of the Religious Society of Friends, London).

will willingly show you and will be able to tell you a lot more about the workers too. I didn't write about the peasants to lead into an advertisement but it has just occurred to me that perhaps some of you would like to … [h]elp the peasants … If so there is a very easy way of doing it. Miss Jordan will either give or send you a parcel of embroideries on approval which you can show to your friends and will give you a percentage of 20% to 25% I believe it is, on anything you sell. There are things of all prices from 1/- upwards – and all kinds, all of them useful: bags, mats, tray clothes, towels, aprons, collars, cushion covers, tea cloths, dresses, jumpers – almost anything you can't think of that can be made from the peasant linen.'

A meeting of different peoples

Margaret's letters about the project are peopled with numerous characters who worked in one way or another with the Women's

Industries. Most of them were members of one of four groups of actors: the international staff; the local staff; the project beneficiaries; and the local power brokers. The members of each group had specific motivations for being involved with the project, and particular expectations of how the work would proceed and their role in it. Margaret was a member of the first group, the international staff, and her letters are written from their perspective. Between the lines, though, we can discern the perspectives of the other three groups.

International altruists

The international field staff who worked for the Friends were all volunteers, and in 1924 they earned only $5.00 a month (roughly US$ 60 in 2010 currency), plus their keep. Most were college educated. Most came on short-term assignments, some for as long as two years. Many of them, including Margaret, stayed less than a year in Poland, before either being reassigned to other Friends' projects or returning home. The fact that they were able to volunteer suggests that they were middle-class people with access to enough money to keep them going without a real salary. Margaret was certainly not wealthy but she must have had some savings. In the middle of her assignment she takes a two-week holiday with friends in Breslau, Germany and then in a hotel in Gloggnitz, Austria and it seems unlikely she funded this out of her $5.00 a month.

Margaret Tregear. Margaret was born into a family of educators and spent most of her life as a teacher and headmistress. Both her grandfather and father were headmasters and all five of her paternal aunts were also teachers, so it seems unlikely that she ever considered any other career. Her father had hoped that all of his seven children would get degrees and be teachers, but in the end only Margaret, the eldest, pursued a career in education. There were only two significant gaps in Margaret's teaching career. She took time off to do relief work with the Friends helping refugees after World War One in 1924–25, and then again after World War Two in 1945–46.

Margaret was raised in a nonconformist family. Her parents were married in a Methodist Chapel and she was listed as a Congregationalist when she entered university. She was not a Quaker at the time she volunteered with the Friends in Poland, but she joined a Quaker Meeting about 10 years later in 1936 when she was teaching on the Isle of Man.

As a teenager she attended Royal Holloway College, a women's college of the University of London. Her father and one aunt had graduated from the same university a generation before. From 1914 she lived and studied in the grand Victorian 'chateau' building which housed the college in rural Surrey. She graduated with a BA Honours in French and English in June 1917. She had an annual scholarship of £30, which her father probably supplemented, but she lived as 'an undergraduate on a shoestring'. She had time for orchestra (she played the viola) and choir, a little tennis and field hockey, and was captain of rowing.

Like many women of her generation Margaret never married. There may be several explanations for this. She came of age at a time when three-quarters of a million British men had been killed in World War One and an equivalent number of women were unlikely to find husbands. But she had also educated herself out of the reach of the vast majority of men. In her day very few men had degrees (for instance, in 1922 only 1,340 men received higher degrees and 360 women out of a population of about 44 million [19]), and few men wanted to marry a woman better educated than themselves. In addition, if she had ambitions to pursue a career in teaching, marriage would have limited her options. Many schools in her era would have rejected a married woman teacher because of the scandalous impossibility of a pregnant woman leading a classroom. In any case, it is not at all clear that Margaret ever demonstrated an aptitude for the compromises which underpin most successful marriages. She was adventurous and she knew what she wanted in life and she pursued it doggedly – a characteristic which made her a useful employee and successful leader, but did not lend itself to the expected demeanour of a wife of the period.

Margaret on horse back, Horodec 1925. *Margaret makes no mention in her letters of riding, so this may be a posed picture. As an urban middle-class woman it seems unlikely she rode before she came to Poland. Behind her is the Catholic Church, a powerful institution driving the Polanization of the Belarusian countryside.*

It says a lot about Margaret's personality, however, that she did not let spinsterhood stand in the way of having a family. In 1929, in a move which was unusual for the time, as a single 32-year-old she adopted an infant boy from Scotland, and raised him as her son. This adoption seems to encapsulate the conflicting nature of her character. While it required a strong-minded woman to embark on a project which must have raised eyebrows in middle-class England, it also shows her intrinsic generosity and desire to make a practical difference in other people's lives. After graduation she had limited contact with the rest of her family for long periods of her life, but she also showed great kindness to her youngest brother and sister, taking them camping, and on European holidays, and at one point bringing her youngest brother to live with her while she taught in Gloucestershire. And when she was older and established running her own school in Switzerland, she made sure her nieces had the adventure of a year or two studying in the memorable atmosphere of the Alps.

Margaret's first international experience was a 'gap year' in 1913–14 studying French in Chalons-sur-Marne, France, before she enrolled in university. After that, for almost half of her working life she worked internationally, starting with the refugee assignment in eastern Poland in the 1920s, teaching in Northern Rhodesia in the 1930s, and in the 1940s doing refugee work in France, Austria, and Germany. She finished the last 15 years of her career from the late 1940s through the early 1960s running a languages school in the Swiss Alps. She had a lifetime fascination with foreign languages and culture, and was proud to maintain long friendships with people in many countries. But her first international job was her position with the Quakers in Horodec.

Altruism and pacifism. The international staff working on the Friends' projects in Poland, and elsewhere, were first and foremost pacifists and idealists, motivated by altruism and humanitarianism to do something to help people in need. Most had lived outside the war zone and so had not been directly affected by the fighting in World War One, but their world had been changed by the war. The pre-war expectations for the trajectories of a middle-class life no longer made sense. They were privileged people, made aware by the realities of war and revolution that their privilege was serendipitous. They were conscious that they bore some responsibility for putting the benefits of their position to use in the wider world. They moved among people with similar outlooks, and expected that most people they worked with would also feel that working to alleviate the suffering of the peasants was an end in itself.

A surprising number of the international volunteers and leaders were women. A biographical dictionary of prominent British women humanitarians of the era shows that these women shared certain characteristics which can be found in many of the women who worked with the Friends on this project, including Margaret. They were early feminists, confident in their own voices and actions; they were well educated; they came from the middle and upper classes; their British identity stood them in good stead as they travelled; politically they often leaned towards the left; they were moved by Christian values; and, they were childless and often single, which freed up their time and energy to work for others. [20]

Conflicting or complementary backgrounds. The first team of international volunteers which arrived in 1919 were all British, but in the following years many Americans joined in the project, as did nationals of other countries including Canada, Australia, Norway and Sweden. [4, 11] The relationship between the British and Americans was not always an easy one, and inevitably cultural differences arose. The AFSC leadership tended to involve a number of active businessmen, experienced in managing large organisations, and sensitive to the benefits of delegating responsibility appropriately. In contrast, the CIS tended to include a larger number of middle-class women with no professional education or experience in business or management. The British CIS committee left administrative decision making to a small executive who seemed reluctant to delegate wide responsibility to the field workers.

'As one member of the English Unit remarked, the prevailing attitude of the American Committee was that of parenthood, ready to let the young men and women it sent out try their wings, while the attitude of the London executive committee tended to be the more restrictive one of spinsterdom, the kindly but authoritative maiden aunt. The American organization was ready to grant a large amount of independence and executive power to its workers in the field, while London was more hesitant in giving this freedom, wished to exercise a more fussy care over its little brood, and sometime to interfere without need.'[8]

Margaret's letters hint at an ongoing saga about renegotiating rental agreements with the different landlords who owned the two houses where the project staff lived and worked. Some of her frustration seemed to result from her inability to make these decisions herself, and the apparent need for the head office in Warsaw and even the committee in London to be involved in what could have been local administrative decisions.

Another difference seems to have been the approach to recruiting project staff. The Americans put more emphasis on choosing people who had technical abilities related to the job they would do, and could be counted on to be 'professional'. The British, on the other hand, were more likely to favour a generalist over a specialist, emphasised character over technical qualifications, and respected the status of the 'amateur'. [8] These differences may have been exacerbated by the fact that, while AFSC representatives were all Quakers, the British organisation was forced to draw from the smaller pool of English Quakers and so included volunteers from other faiths. As one American Quaker noted 'The British seem to have selected unique and odd people who are against war but do not understand the ways of Quakers and so there is friction even among us workers'. [13] Margaret herself was not a Quaker, although she did become a member 10 years later in England.

Over the 10 previous years of operations the English organization had fielded more than 1,000 volunteers across their European units. Candidates were selected by a London committee, and the committee did not always find it easy to recognise how well a potential volunteer would adapt to the range of challenges encountered in field work. [14] An American working in Horodec six months before Margaret arrived, observed a telling staffing failure.

'One day a new girl was brought to the outpost at Horodec to help with the Women's Industries. She was English, looked a little young for the situation, and was somewhat on the fat side. About the first or second day, and out of a clear sky, as it were, she announced to me "I only eat fruits and nuts". To this remarkable statement I said nothing at all, but couldn't help wondering where such items were to come from, since I had never seen any of the sort around here, and we were glad to take whatever we got.

For four days she spent her entire time writing letters to her friends back in England, telling them where she was and, I suppose, describing her surroundings. Then suddenly the office in Warsaw called her in and, we heard later, shipped her back to England.

I have no idea how this all happened so fast. The wonder is that the authorities ever sent her out there in the first place; obviously they had no conception of field conditions. I couldn't help feeling sorry for the girl: she was probably back home before her friends had received her letters! At least she had proof of where she had been!' [4]

Margaret, on the other hand, seemed – at least most of the time – to enjoy the variety of challenges the project threw at her, and took pride in making the most of the lifestyle presented by rudimentary rural living conditions, alternating with nights at the opera in Warsaw.

Local pragmatists

There were not enough international staff to carry out all the work of the mission, and significantly, many of the international staff did not speak the local languages. To implement the projects on a large scale and to work effectively with the beneficiaries, all the projects needed intermediary local staff. The local staff also worked for $4.00, $5.00 and $6.00 a month, but for them this amount of money was closer to a real salary, although probably not enough to support a family. They seem to have been educated middle-class men and women who had come down in the world, and faced great economic uncertainty since the war. They were not starving like the peasants, but they were not far removed from it.

Many of the local men hired were Russian ex-army officers in their late 20s or early 30s. They had ended the wars fighting on the side of the Russian White Army against the Bolsheviks during the Russian civil war, and were stranded exiles in Poland, unable to go home to the Soviet Union or contact their families. These local employees were mostly realists motivated by pragmatism. Despite the low salary, they needed their jobs badly and had few prospects when they were finally let go. [4, 14]

The local women working with Margaret were all Polish, middle-class educated women, who likewise needed the job. A few like Sophia Wrzeszcz, had options. Sophia was fluently multilingual, and the daughter of a Polish army officer who had the connections to eventually leave for America to work for a Polish consulate. Alternatively, there is Ms Czarnecka whose story unfolds over two letters. She was a refugee who has endured some serious trauma in the past couple of years. She is described as being rather scatterbrained in her approach to her work, and Margaret is disappointed that she doesn't embrace 'the spirit' of the project – as Margaret defines it – and lacks practical skills. She was quickly let go but she found the loss of the job devastating, however unsuited she may have been for it. Margaret's understanding of her Polish colleagues real motivations was limited by language. Apart from Sophia, none of the other women Margaret worked with had good foreign language skills, and Margaret only spoke French and a little German. It becomes clear through the letters that while Margaret was happy to talk about her Polish colleagues in her letters, she actually had some difficulty talking with them.

Margaret's letters reveal mixed feelings about her Polish colleagues and she admits that at times she finds her local staff as a bit annoying. On the positive side they are 'friendly', 'pleasant', 'sociable, and jolly', with 'charming manners'. At work they can be 'methodical', 'conscientious and reliable'. Some of them turn out to be 'gay and energetic', and of 'much temperament and resource'. But at the same time Margaret can't help commenting on how they seem more emotional and changeable than she is used to. When under pressure the Poles seem to be 'fussing', 'feverish', 'in trembling dither', distracted by 'nervous energy' and 'filled with apprehension', or even 'rushing around in an affairée manner'. They certainly don't follow rules, instructions or schedules in the way that an English woman would expect. And when things go wrong she finds them 'resigned', 'disconsolate', 'injured', and they may even 'cultivate the martyr' or be 'subject to the blackest depths of despondency'. With one particular local staff member, Margaret admits that "...her ineffable resignation is irritating to the last degree".

Desperate beneficiaries

Communications were even more difficult with the Belarusian peasants. The Belarusian language may be considered a dialect of Russian and has some overlap with Polish. But, it seems that few of the local staff working with the Friends were fluent in Belarusian and none of them came from a peasant background. Margaret's letters contain various direct quotes from the peasant women who join in the project activities, but in fact it seems likely that much of what they said was translated loosely at best. We have to wonder how many of the disputes that erupted between the Belarusian women and Margaret were created or exacerbated by the inadequate translation provided by the Polish women caught in the middle.

Desperation was what motivated the Belarusian peasants to participate in the project. When the Friends arrived in their area they were literally starving, and even after harvesting the next year's crops their poverty was profound and hunger and disease were constantly in the background. By 1925 all of them had lived through 10 yeas of economic uncertainty and powerlessness, and had had a lifetime of experience with the arbitrary exercise of power. Their expectations for the project were low, and Margaret comments on the resignation with which some of them greeted their wages – or indeed their lack of wages, when the unintelligible record

Sceptical participants. *These women in front of their dugout home are typical project beneficiaries, with no power and few resources beyond their skill with needle and thread. They approached the project with scepticism and often left puzzled by the incomprehensible rules devised by the foreign administrators.*

cards of the Friends implied that they had 'stolen' embroidery thread. Their life experience had not led them to expect justice, or even a fair wage, so many of them took what little they got from the project in silence. Others protested in vain when they hit up against Margaret's unbending British adherence to the 'rule of law', as defined by the project guidelines and the record cards.

Margaret struggled with her inability to bridge the cultural distance between herself and the Belarusian peasants. All too often she slips into a patronizing tone. She sees them as 'big and rather naughty children', comic and 'so stupid that they are unconsciously funny'. They 'don't know their surnames', they have 'no idea of arranging their time', they 'talk loudly' and 'all at the same time', and they seem 'like a herd of cows' crowding into the office. Sometimes she finds them 'primitive' and 'crude', and when she gets into a conflict with them they 'loose their tempers' and become 'indignant', 'abusive', and they swear or are 'pathetic and weep'. It frustrated her that they seemed to be 'no respecters of persons of authority'. At other times they seem 'afraid', or 'incapable of being stirred', 'stolid and inert', they 'stand and stare', 'impassive'. And 'hardly anyone says thank you'.

On the other hand, Margaret respected that the peasants are 'very patient' and finds them 'very likeable with a great sense of humour'. They are skilled workers who do 'real interpretive art' when they 'illustrate all they see' with their needles and thread. Others are 'dignified and capable' and 'show great friendliness'. They are people with a 'simple dignity, strong independence, and love of the soil'. The depth of her conflicted feelings is most evident when she describes how the young loom girls 'all kiss one's hand on saying good night which I think is a perfectly awful plan, and causes me the most acute discomfort'. She wants to like and respect these people and yet she can't help but feel uncomfortable among them.

Manipulative power brokers

By 1924 the Friends were treading a difficult tight rope with the Polish government, and needed the support of good political connections to offset growing prejudice and suspicion about their motives from some quarters, in particular the Catholic Church. Two of the most prominent Polish politicians of the 1920s make cameo appearances in Margaret's letters. The complicated national political scene in Poland in the 1920s was characterized by a revolving door of changing governments in Warsaw. In the spring of 1925 Wladyslaw Grabski was in power and Józef Pilsudski was out, but their positions had been reversed earlier and would be again in only a few months.

Józef Pilsudski wandered by the Women's Industries stall at the Kobryn Exhibition in 1925, and spent some time considering a piece of handiwork. Pilsudski was probably the most famous man in Poland and was hailed by many as the modern founder of Poland. Having helped establish independence in 1918, and having led the Polish army through the Polish-Soviet War 1919–21, he dominated politics through to 1923. While he was pursuing the war, a member of the Quaker's London Committee met with him and attempted to persuade him to end the war through negotiation, but had no success. In 1925 he was technically in retirement, but was still exerting considerable influence in the backrooms of politics. In May 1926 he led a coup and took control of the country. He then remained in various positions of power until he died in 1935.

Wladyslaw Grabski had been prime minister for one month in 1920 and was again Prime Minister between December 1923 and November 1925. Margaret's brush with Grabski occurred when his secretary attended a meeting of the KPPKW. The Friends had set up the KPPKW to localise – at least in theory – the management of their relief program. To increase the committee's chances of success they invited Polish government officials to participate. Grabski was a member of the Advisory Committee set up to oversee the Kolpin Orphanage and Agricultural School. The school was designed by the Friends to be a legacy of their work in the country and was the first agricultural school in the Polesia province. Margaret pondered why the prime minister would think it worth his time (or even his secretary's time) to participate in what was a very small relief program, relative to the huge economic and political crises Poland faced in the 1920s. It is possible he was influenced by his government's concern to be seen to be reaching out to the large minority populations, including the one million Belarusians who had been swept into the new Poland following the Polish-Soviet War. Or perhaps he was intrigued by the committee's plans to make a model of the agricultural training school at Kolpin. After resigning as prime minister he followed his personal interest in agricultural education as the rector of the Warsaw Agricultural University for most of the rest of his life. [4, 18]

While the Warsaw Unit cultivated national political connections, Margaret committed herself to cultivating the local power brokers in Horodec who included the Vojt (the head of the district administration), the commandant (probably the police chief), various Soltys (mayors of local villages), the school master and mistress, the railway station master, and the local estate owners. She was aware that the success of the project might depend on the support it received from the people who represented the state at the local level, most of whom are Polish. For instance, the Friends frequently used the local Soltys to round up the Belarusian peasant women they worked with or to put pressure on any women who had not returned their embroidery work. On their side, these local officials were in a tenuous position. They represented a new Polish state which was struggling to gain legitimacy against the background of an unstable and corrupt government in Warsaw. And they represented a new imperial force, which aspired to Polanize the local Belarusian population. These local officials main interest in the project was probably the potential it gave them for leverage over the local population, or for the prestige that came with being the partner of a foreign agency.

The Jewish population are almost absent from Margaret's letters, although they formed a major part of the Horodec population and made up most of the local tradesmen and business people. Only Mr Vinograd, the landlord, is mentioned and even he is not named until the last letter. The Jewish population of Polesia lived predominantly in the towns and made up a quarter of the population of Horodec and half of Drohiczyn before the war. They always had a tenuous relationship with the government, although local accounts suggest that the Tsarist administration was more light handed than the Polish one which replaced it. The Jewish population was not forced to evacuate during the war and although 200,000 left eastern Poland for Russia, [11] many stayed on in the villages like Horodec and Drohiczyn. Despite living on or near the front lines, and having to shelter in bunkers while the Germans and Russians lobbed shells over their heads, and being targeted by pogroms during the Polish-Soviet war, the majority of the Jewish population survived World War One period better than the Belarusian peasants, more than half of whom died as a result of the evacuation. Like the peasants, many Jews lost their houses when the towns were burned, but they had the advantage of being able to rebuild earlier. By 1925 they had re-established their homes and trades, but they suffered from the same economic uncertainty as the rest of Poland, with the added unease about increasing anti-Semitism. [1, 3, 4]

Far flung readers

Margaret considered her letters a kind of journal where she could frankly record her experiences on this new assignment. She wrote to women friends who obviously knew her well enough that she felt she could be honest about the ups and downs of her journey. These readers were all women, mostly single, and obviously they could read English. They were scattered across Europe, in England, France, Holland, and Germany. Some seem to have been English, as they have the title Miss, but there is one Mademoiselle and two Frauleins. We get the impression some of these women knew each other, and the final letter suggests that some of them plan to meet in September (possibly in Marseilles). Their addresses were handwritten on the typed carbon copies of the letters which suggests that they are not necessarily all the readers and that another copy of the letters may have been sent to a second list. Their names were:

Miss D.A. Wilkinson, Gainsborough House, Bolton Lane, Ipswich, UK
Miss Cotton
Mlle. A. Strousser, 33 Grande rue, Briey, Meurthe et Moselle, France

Frl. Else Stenzel, Bognslavitz, Post Kaltern, Krs., Breslau, Germany, and later Muller str 50, Munchen, Germany

Frl. K. Gombert, Greenblum??, Shodehnen, Krs. Darkehne??

Mrs. Straus, Essenweinsts, 4th, Nurnberg, Germany

Miss G.A. Giles, bei Frau Dr. Dietzschold, Lanterensts 37th, Mainz, Germany,

Miss A. Gallois, Bankastrand, gg., The Hague, Holland

Dr. B. M. Smyth, C.M.S. Hospital, Multan Cantonment, Punjab, India

Kathleen Lodge, England

Miss Ada Jordan, Devonshire House, 136 Bishopsgate, London, E.C., UK

And now, many years later, we too become readers of these letters.

xx xxx xx

Dr Beatrice Marion Smyth (1894–1965). Beatrice was born in Orlando, Florida to an American father and an English mother. She left the US to live with her mother's family in England when she was 13. Her mother's family had a tradition of working in medicine: her grandfather was a doctor and her aunt a midwife. Beatrice started her medical studies in 1917 and registered as a doctor in February 1924. She began working at the Church Missionary Society Women's Hospital at Multan in the Punjab around the same time that Margaret went to Poland. It appears she never married but continued to work in India for much of her career. She moved to the CEZ Hospital at Rainawari, Srinagar, in the Kashmir in the 1930s and she returned to England in 1948 after the Independence of India, aged 54. She lived and was buried in Worthing, Sussex, at the age of 71 in 1965.

Ada Jordan 1893–1991. Ada was christened with the German name Margarete Gertrude Ada, but she went by the more English Ada for all her life. She was born in Hertfordshire, England just after her family emigrated from Germany so that her father could take up a position as curator at the new Natural History Museum in Tring. Ada's father came to have quite a British outlook, but her mother remained stoically German all her life, and Ada must have dealt with some conflicting feelings during World War One. While she worked in London, Ada was heavily involved with the Friends work in Poland starting in 1920. She was the main person responsible for the sales in England of the products of the Women's Industries imported from Poland, and she became the secretary responsible for Poland, for the Russia and Poland Committee of the CIS in 1924. She remained involved with this work through the 1930s, and in 1932 was able to visit the project. In the 1940s she again worked for the renamed Friends' Relief Service. She lived to the age of 98. [21]

One Englishwoman's Account

List of characters

International Staff

From the Friends' Head Office in London

A. Ruth Fry (47) - General Secretary of the Friends' War Victims Relief Committee, from 1914 to 1924 (UK b.1878-d.1962)

Florence M. Barrow (49) - Former head of the Friends' Relief Mission to Poland from 1921 to 1924 (UK b.1876-d.1964)

T. Edmond Harvey (50) - Visiting on behalf of the Council for International Service (CIS), Retired politician (UK b.1875-d.1955)

William A. Albright (73) - Former Vice-Chairman of the Friends' War Victims Relief Committee, visiting on behalf of the CIS (UK b.1852-d.1942)

Henry Harris - CIS, arriving to take Wilmer Young's place, heads the Friends' work in Poland from August 1925 (UK)

Ada Jordan (32) - Managing the sales of the products of the Women's Industries in England, from the early 1920s through the 1930s, and from 1924 was a joint secretary of the CIS Russia and Poland Committee in London in 1925 (UK b.1893-d.1991)

At the Friends Office in Warsaw

Wilmer J. Young (38) - Head of the Friends' Relief Mission to Poland, from June 1924 to July 1925 (US b.1887-d.1983) with his wife Mildred (US b. 1901-d.1955) and baby Margaret

Jane S. Pontefract (34) - Quaker volunteer in Poland from 1920, and General Manager of the Women's Industries in Poland from 1924 to 1929 (UK b.1891-d.1946)

At the Friends Outpost in Horodec

Muriel Heagney (39) - Previous manager of the Women's Industries in

Horodec, February-December 1924 (AU b.1885-d.1974)

Margaret Tregear (27) - Manager of the Women's Industries in Horodec, October 1924–August 1925 (UK b.1897-d.1984)

Hilda Buckmaster (28) - Next manager of the Women's Industries in Horodec, starting August 1925 (UK b.1897-d.1993)

Richard R. Taylor (24) - American in charge of the sawmills, (US b.1901-d.1974)

At Kolpin Agricultural School and Orphanage, Stradecz

Erling Kjekstad (30) - Controller, (Norwegian b.1895-d?)

Local Staff

At the Friends Office in Warsaw

Mrs. Ewa Henoch - Working on the Women's Industries with Jane Pontefract

Mrs. Jenycz - Working on the Women's Industries with Jane Pontefract

Ladislas 'Skora' Skoraczewski - Volunteer and translator since 1919 (UK/Polish), married to an American Quaker, Grace Hoff

At the Friends Outpost in Horodec

Sophia Wrzeszcz - Polish worker/translator for the Women's Industries from March 1924-March 1925

Miss Wrzeszcz - Sophia's sister who replaces her when she leaves for America

Miss Stankiewicz (35) - Polish worker in the Women's Industries

Miss Golonowska (23) - Polish worker in the Women's Industries

Miss Czarnecka (30) Polish worker in the Women's Industries

Potonia - Head stable man

At Kolpin Agricultural School and Orphanage, Stradecz

Jadwiga Bialowieska - Volunteer and translator since 1919, and Head of the Orphanage from 1924-1926 (UK/Polish)

Mr. Maluta - Polish

Local Power Brokers

In Warsaw

Wladyslaw Grabski (51) - Prime Minister of Poland 1923-1925 and member of the KPPKW (b.1874-d.1938)

Józef Pilsudski (58) - Prominent political and military leader of Poland, temporarily out of office (b.1867-d.1935)

In Horodec

The Vojt - Head of the district administration, or Gmina, in Horodec

The Commandant - Probably the local Police Chief

The Starosta - Community elder from the town of Kobryn

The Soltys - Mayors of local villages

The Djieciatne - Headman of a hamlet, responsible for about 10 households

The Priest - Catholic Priest and landlord of the house the women live in

The Jew - Haim-Nisl Vinograd, landlord of house the women use for 'distributions' and work

His son (17) - Abraham Vinograd

Mr. Andronowski - A Polish estate owner at Horodec

Antoni Wyslouch (61) - A Polish estate owner at Drohiczyn (b.1864-d.1940)

Beneficiaries

At the Friends Outpost in Horodec

Vera Kurylowicz (18) - A Belorussian orphan who lives in the house in Horodec and works as a weaver (b.1907–d.??)

At Kolpin Agricultural School and Orphanage, Stradecz

Jacob 'Yashka' Gryn (12) - A Belorussian orphan who is a student in the agriculture programme (b.1913–d.??)

4 December 1924, Warsaw

Margaret was officially appointed to her new position by the Russia and Poland Committee of the Committee for International Service (CIS) in London on 30 September 1924. She began her journal letters soon after she arrived in Poland in October 1924, but the first letters in the series have been lost. This may be the fifth letter as the next letter is labelled 'Instalment 6'.

Margaret left England just after the beginning of October and travelled to Warsaw via the Hague. On the 20th she was in Warsaw for her first meeting with the KPPKW. By the first week of November she was in Horodec getting to know her new Polish co-workers and being oriented to the workings of the project by her predecessor Muriel Heagney, and in the second week she took on her first 'distribution'.

We join Margaret after as she is making her first return trip to Warsaw. During her visit she gets to know the English Quaker managing the Women's Industries from Warsaw, Jane Pontefract, and Wilmer Young, a volunteer from AFSC who is the current Head of the Friends Relief Mission to Poland. Margaret helps represent the project at a Handicrafts Exhibition and enjoys a night at the opera.

My journal has got a bit behind, as I have been in Warsaw since Saturday.

I had quite a decent journey down [from Horodec to Warsaw] as the seat next to me was empty so that I could curl up and doze at intervals; but I never met anything like the heat on these trains; door and windows tight shut, - the latter nailed up for the winter and boiling hot water pipes all the way along under the seat, – it is exactly like what I imagine a Turkish bath to be – and the smells are wonderful in their variety. But it would be still more uncomfortable to freeze. The train starts at eight and gets to Warsaw at half past five in the morning; it is only 236 km but the trains are very slow, and stop at most stations for quite a long rest. It was very dark and misty when I arrived, much more like evening than morning; I found I had quite revised my opinion of Warsaw Doroskas, after riding in the Kobryn ones and in the furmanka, and I thoroughly enjoyed the long ride to the flat, and marvelled at the sight of tall stone houses once more. In fact I got every ounce of enjoyment out of all the strange things of civilization, - water that is not yellow, and drinkable, running out of a real tap, electric light, a gas ring, bells, and all the things one takes for granted as a rule. I had a bath, my first since leaving Warsaw, (though I have since then been told that the receptacle used for washing linen in the wash shed here is a zinc bath in which it would be possible to tub) and tumbled into bed. Marja [the maid] woke me at nine with breakfast, and soon after Jane Pontefract came in in her dressing gown and sat on the other bed and talked. She is an awfully nice soul, exactly like her name, I think; very down right and business like, thoroughly knowing her own mind without wanting to settle every one else's for them, accustomed I should imagine, to carrying through anything she undertook, and quite undaunted by any physical conditions; and with it all rather sensitive and shy underneath.

We got up in time for Meeting at twelve. There were only half a dozen people there but two men from an interesting village community somewhere on the Russian border. They call themselves "Christians in the Spirit" and for the last twenty three years have been running their community exactly on the lines of the early Quakers. The movement was started by a Baptist minister, and they were visited by a teacher from another similar group further south, but apart from that these peasants themselves have evolved their ideas. They are pacifists, refuse to take oaths, have much the same form of worship, except they include hymns, and consider themselves jointly responsible for relieving poverty etc. in their midst. Jane Pontefract is experimenting to see if it will be possible for them to work up a co-operative system of embroidering; they to buy their cottons from us and we to take their finished work, but otherwise for them to run it on their own. The problem yet to be solved is whether they can do any embroidery worth having; I do hope they can, it will be an interesting experiment if they can; - besides Jane feels that it might give her or some one else an opportunity of enlightening them on what will happen if they continue to intermarry among themselves, as there are only 170 of them; the men may, but are not encouraged to, take a wife from outside their community, but the women are not allowed to marry outside themselves.

After lunch we went to call for Wilmer Young and then on to tea with an Irish lady, married to a Pole, and professor of English at the University. She was a most priceless person; quite unbelievable like the heroine of a romantic novel. Her hair, dark blue eyes, complexion, her whole appearance were host of a typical colleen picture, and her vivacious manner was all the more piquant since she is beginning to forget her English, and has adopted various continental gestures. She was delightfully amusing, - a born teacher I should think, and heart and soul in her work. The housing shortage is as bad in Warsaw as anywhere and they only have one room, but it is a most lofty, spacious apartment, simply beautifully furnished. The table was laden with the most thrilling eatables, but that was really rather tantalising, because our hostess ate nothing at all herself and offered us nothing after the first round, so to speak, and we sat for simply hours in front of fascinating biscuits, chocolates, plum cake and a special kind of dough nuts, without sampling anything except the later. Don't you think that was une vraie tragédie?

Most of Mrs. Hermanova's students are Jews, and we finished up with a discussion as to whether it would be possible for them to use the English reading room that is being started at Widok [the Friend's Warsaw office address], without the chance of being insulted by the other members. I think Jane and Wilmer Young are going to try to find some way of guaranteeing that, but for the present, they had to say that they couldn't be sure. The feeling against Jews and treatment of them as a race absolutely apart is stronger here than in Germany even, and certainly their type is even more marked. I don't know what the proportion is but it seems as if there are quite as many Jewish as Polish people in Poland.

We went back to supper at the Young's, - and after that went to get a Puhar (pronounced Poo-ha; it does sound very Gilbert and Sullivanish, doesn't it? -) she had been talking of this ever since my arrival, and mystifying me by talking of tall ones and short ones etc., but from something Mrs. [Mildred] Young said, I jumped to what it was. "Oh, is it a Sundae?" I asked, and Jane, who is slightly deaf, and who thought her Sabbatarian principles were being attacked, drew herself up and said indignantly, "Well! It's only a restaurant!" She is evidently less acquainted with such things in England than in Poland, for a Sundae it turned out to be, but of a wonderful decorative variety, hitherto unrevealed to my experience. Tall biscuits, three times as high as the rest, with graceful curves at the top, stood in the middle and smaller ones round the sides, it really was delicious.

After this we all went to see off an ex-mission member [Grace Hoff] who was going back to America for a holiday, and to get better, as she has been ill. She is married to a Pole [Ladislas Skoraczewski], apparently there were a larger number of causalities in the Polish field in the Mission than anywhere else; I have heard a rumour that 49% succumbed, but have no idea as to how authentic that statistic is! On Monday evening Jane invited the sorrowing husband in to play Bridge, and as they couldn't get a fourth we played three handed.

Monday I spent at the Office, going through various things that had to be talked over, and helping unpack and price things for the exhibition; I also packed my Christmas parcel and sent it off, - I do hope it will arrive in time. They usually take about three weeks so there isn't a great deal of margin.

Tuesday morning I went shopping with Mrs. Jenycz, working steadily through a long list of all kinds of things. I have just discovered to my great grief that the dust pans which we bought in a hurry have a gap of about an inch between the pan and the floor; it never dawned on my benighted intelligence that there could be such a thing as one with a curved edge. So one we have tried to bend into shape and the other I shall have to take down with me next time to change. Hitherto our method of getting rid of dust has been a novel one; you sweep up a moderate proportion of the dust in the room into a heap, pick up most of it in your hands and throw it over the sill into the next room, disperse the remainder preferably where it is not too visible, and so on until you reach the outside door.

On Tuesday evening, Mrs. Young, two of the weirdest freaks you ever saw in the shape of two Australian ladies, Jane Pontefract, and I went to Lohengrin. The Opera house is quite small for such a big place and was nothing like full, possibly because of Wagner being German, I don't know, and people used the Overture as a sociable accompaniment for them to get to their places. I loved the music and the orchestra was quite good, but the soloists and the chorus were nothing to write home about. Nurnberg Opera beat this hollow. Some of the softer effects of the chorus were beautiful, but I am quite certain that where they join in the quintet before the fight, the five, the chorus, and the orchestra were in entirely different keys. It was excruciating.

The staging was beautiful and so were the colours of the costumes but of course all the principals were ancient and stout, and the swan was the most priceless thing you have ever seen. Whoever designed it had evidently never seen a live one swim. It was right up out of the water; if only they hadn't wanted to make it look real, it might have passed muster, but it wriggled its neck at intervals in what looked like an agonizing appeal for biscuits, and the cotton wool it was made of wrinkled in rings round its neck. In the intervals, Miss Von Heinerbucklel reminisced. She once spent a weekend at Wagner's house, where her hostess, having once received her, left her severely to her own devices (and really, looking at Miss Von H. one feels that it was understandable, even if inexcusable), and she says that she is connected with all the celebrities, one has ever heard of. She filled me with an insane desire to giggle when she fixed me with her eye and made some arch remark; bushy curly brown wig, comes down nearly to her equally bushy eyebrows, obviously coloured up to match, and she has that sort of double chin which hangs down in a festoon and does duty for neck as well.

Yesterday morning, after being treated to breakfast in bed after our evening's dissipation, I called at the office and then made my way to the Exhibition. In case I haven't explained before, it is an exhibition of all kinds of hand work made by Polish women, but there seemed to be trade stalls as well and on the whole it was rather like a swish church bazaar than anything else. All the Warsaw ladies who were anybody were congregated there, gossiping or rushing round in a fearfully affairée manner, according as to whether they were ready or not. Most were not! The affair opened at five, and at half past six the stall next to ours wasn't finished.

Just before five a paper ribbon was tied across the entrance, and various people were shooed to the other side of it, Jane and myself among the others, when to our cold horror we saw the Cardinal arrived through the door opposite up, and all the Committee ladies introduced in turn curtseying low, and kissing his Eminence's hand. I longed to turn tail under the paper ribbon again, and various people were bobbing backwards and forwards, and pleaded with Jane in impassioned undertones, but though she was also suffering from dire panic lest the dread moment should arrive, she was made of sterner mettle, and stood her ground; merciful Providence intervened, because, having reached the middle of the room, the Cardinal and his train paused for tea, and on returning to see that the stall was all right I discovered from the chief lady fusser, - I don't know who she was but evidently the leading dame on the executive side, - that if we were selling we ought to stay by our stall. So we were on the safe side of the line when the Cardinal continued his journey. We wondered what would happen when he got near our stall as the Princess who was piloting him round knows Jane perfectly well and is sympathetic to the work, but has to conceal the fact for political reasons as she represents the [Roman Catholic] party. Here again luck was with us, as the people next to us seized on the Cardinal, and the Princess was able to avoid introducing him or outing us. She sounded quite a friendly and charming soul, and had no obviously royal signs about her.

I had begun to feel quite thrilled at having found the hall all by myself and going by various tram routes to different places in the city, but it was nothing to the pride I felt having safely dealt with driver, porter and having bought my own ticket on the homeward journey. I was lucky enough to get one of those chopped off compartments with the seat on one side only, all to myself most of the way. I could lie down all night, but I did not dare to go right off to sleep with about £75 in the kit bag over my head and men popping in and out all night. They climb along the footboard, in one door and out of the other. The ones who did come in were the ticket collectors, a man to see about the heating, and another to renew the candles, but that is also the way train thieves manage too.

Not the bandits, - they simply hold up the train and go right through it, collecting money, and clothes; if I met any of these I think I should be particularly careful not to cross them, and make them quite welcome even to the £75, but the other people seize their opportunity chiefly when passengers are asleep. I really should be scared to death if a raid did come off, - the only consolation would be that one could talk about it for the rest of one's natural life, even inventing a truly heroic role, for there would be no evidence to the contrary. I shouldn't be at all surprised if Jane doesn't meet them one of these times, she has a three hours drive across the very country they are attending to, and the man who drives them is absolutely terrified if they don't arrive before dusk; she is known to take down regular sums of money for the distribution too. They have sent notices to the two big estates owners in her district announcing their intention of paying a call, and they generally keep their work. It sounds just like a tale of Corsica or somewhere like that; the bandits arrive, sup with the family, and after the meal the stuff is politely handed over. Whether the estate owners are too intimidated to make proper preparation I don't know; but the idea of announcing their visit shows what stage things are at. There is a rumour that when the last big lot were caught it was because the Police were on strike for a larger share!

I can quite imagine Jane telling them what she thinks of them though, if ever she comes across them.

xx xxx xx

Jane Sylvia Gertrude Pontefract (1891–1976) Born into a Quaker family in Dringhouses, York, in 1891, Jane had two brothers 12 and 13 years older than her. She studied at the Quaker's Ackworth School for five years. She first volunteered to work with the Friends during WWI at a convalescent home in France before transferring to Poland in 1920 where she worked for 10 more years. She took over responsibility for the Women's Industries project in 1923 and managed the Polish end of this work until she returned to England to live with her parents at Dringhouses in 1930. She re-visited the Women's Industry project three times in 1932, 1934 and 1936. She continued to live in Dringhouses until her death in 1976 at the age of 84. [21, 22]

Wilmer J. Young (1887–1983) and Mildred Binns Young (1901–1995) Born into a Quaker family in Iowa, Wilmer attended Quaker Schools and was a graduate of Haverford College. Wilmer began working for AFSC in Verdun, France as a conscientious objector during World War One, and went on to join the work in Poland after the war with his wife Mildred. Mildred was born in Ohio and graduated from Western Reserve University. In 1925, aged 38, Wilmer was the Head of the Warsaw Unit of the Friends Relief Mission and in 1925 and 1926 he helped organise two German-Polish peace conferences. When he returned to the US he worked as a math teacher for several years. In 1936 Mildred and he moved to the southern States where they spent many years working for AFSC with poor share-croppers and tenant farmers. Mildred wrote several pamphlets inspired by this work which are still in print. Later in life Wilmer gave his full time to the peace action movement and in his 70s he was arrested for civil disobedience as an anti-nuclear missile activist more than once. He died aged 95. [23, 24]

7 December 1924, Horodec

This letter was written in two rounds, and this second part is written from Horodec where we join Margaret as she picks up a continuing saga about renegotiating the rent for their living quarters with the Priest who owns the house. Margaret has her first meeting with local government and realises the project needs better local public relations. The woman Margaret is replacing in Horodec, Muriel Heagney is spending her last few days at the outpost to brief Margaret before she leaves. Another AFSC volunteer, Richard Taylor, is also leaving and a new Polish worker, Miss Stankiewicz, joins the team, so we begin to see how rapid staff turnover is one of the challenges for everyone involved with the project. Sophia Wrzeszcz however, has been in Horodec since the spring of 1924 at least, and provides some continuity and vital language skills.

The vicissitudes of the dealings with the Priest and the old lady are simply legion; the Priest made an offer at the beginning of the week to arrange things with his successor if we would pay him 20 zloty a month. By Thursday he had shifted his ground and threatened us with legal proceedings unless by today we had agreed to start paying him that at once, on the grounds that the contract was made with the Mission which no longer exists. Technically he is right because the contract was made three years ago was signed by a member of the agricultural section which has now liquidated; morally he has no right at all, and legally I think he would have a very weak case, as he made the new agreement with Muriel Heagney who represented the Industries, and who explained him the whole situation in the presence of a reliable witness, and in his last letter but two he states that the recognises himself in honour bound by the last renewal of the contract. We are gaining time by referring the matter to the Committee in Warsaw, but it is very possible we shall have to make some new arrangement with his successor. [page(s) missing]

I brought back the lamp from Warsaw for the loom room, and gave it to Vera [Kurylowicz], the loom girl who lives here, to take down the next morning; and when we came across to breakfast, we found all the girls waiting here, having been driven out by the old woman. She has tried to beat them, and actually did give one of the girls a big whack on the head later, but I suspect they were really more afraid of her violent tongue, for after having waited while we had breakfast, they decided of their own accord, not to wait until we could go back with them but to return by themselves. Nothing worse than oration from the old woman has happened since, but nobody feels that we are at the end of our troubles with her.

I do think we made a step forward on Friday, however, when we went to see the Vojt, who is the head municipal man. Somehow it seems that no-one had got in touch with the responsible officials before, and Muriel Heagney went to say her farewell and introduce me, incidentally explaining all about the work of the Industries. She conducted the interview very well indeed, and the Vojt was most sensible to deal with. He told us quite frankly that the general feeling was that we were occupying house room, needed for more important purposes, and the little amount of work we gave the women did not appear to compensate for that; he was very careful to say that he was not expressing his own opinion, but at the same time did not say that he disagreed with this. So we told him how much we were actually paying out and how many women were getting employment, and he said that if we ever needed his help and cooperation he would be willing to give it. We also made it quite clear what relationship the Industries and the Polish Committee [Komitet Pomocy Polskim Kresom Wschodnim, (KPPKW)] in Warsaw bear to the old Mission. That was all the more amusing because the interview was taking place in the only room at the Gmina [local government office], with heaps of people round drinking in the whole of our conversation, and just as we were embarked on this explanation the Priest came in and got our legal position explained to him gratis.

However, it made us realise that we are too cut off from the people of the place and we decided to see that the leading people had copies of the various reports and were kept in touch with the work. Sophia Wrzeszcz has ideas on working a local advisory committee, and is going to submit a memorandum to Warsaw on the subject. Theoretically there is a good deal to be said in favour, but practically, unless they are tactfully chosen and handled, I think that they sometimes create more difficulties than they give help.

Another bright idea that came to us this afternoon is that of giving over the room in the house where we sleep that has hitherto been used as an office for the saw mills. Although we could very well do with it for a sitting room, we don't actually need it, and that would pacify the police, and possibly compensate us for anything we have to pay the Priest when we finally come to an agreement with him.

I do hope you aren't all thoroughly bored with the history of our various negotiations. They take up such a large share of our time and thought that it hardly seems possible to write a journal at all and leave them out.

We have just seen Miss Heagney off; she is going on to Russia for some weeks after about a week in Warsaw, and we are feeling a very depleted party, for Richard Taylor left on Thursday. He was going down to Warsaw by train that crossed the one in which I came up, and I just had time for a hasty good bye, and to wave a parting hanky after him. The other two had gone to Drohiczyn and Potonia was the only other one to see him off; he was frightfully cut up, as he thought no end of Richard.

The other member of our party is a Miss Stankiewicz, who has come to do the housekeeping and weaving. She is very methodical, and will be very reliable I think. She is about 35 or more I imagine and wears the air of a resigned and worthy soul determinedly making the best of things, - though if you ask of what I am sure I don't know, nor would she! But a drooping chin, and a deprecating manner give one that impression. I have hardly got to know her at all yet, because she doesn't talk English, and therefore hasn't been able to join in at table. She is very slow at understanding French, - my brand at any rate, and I find it difficult to realize that anyone with as good an accent and intonation as hers (Polish intonation is awfully like French, and the accent seems to come naturally to them) can be ignorant of the simplest vocabulary. But from now on our common language will, I suppose be French, and I shall hear more of her.

By the way, talking of pronunciation, one or two people have been curious to know how to pronounce Sophia Wrzeszcz's name. I can't write it in phonetics for the benefit of the initiated, because I've forgotten the sign for ch, so I'll put it down in English letters, except for the second which is pronounced like the j in French je, jaune, etc. It's quite a tongue twister of a name; - Vjeshtch to get into one syllable.

I am expecting to have a very busy week, taking everything over and collecting my wits about things, and then on Friday I am going down to Warsaw again for two Committees, Industries on Saturday, and General on Monday; quite soon after that Christmas will be upon us. I am probably going to spend that, with Jane Pontefract at Kolpin, the agricultural school and orphanage, and she is going to come back here for the weekend after Boxing Day.

Very best Christmas wishes to everyone this reaches in time and love from Margaret.

xx xxx xx

Vera Kurylowicz (1907–??) Vera was born into a Belorussian peasant family in a village near Brest. She and her three sisters grew up on a 14 acre farm with a cottage, orchard and livestock. When in 1915 her family were ordered to evacuate by the retreating Tsarist army, they left with one cart and some livestock. The livestock were requisitioned by the army, and the horse and cart sold before they boarded a train for Russia. When they reached the Samara Oblast, her mother and one sister died of typhoid. Her father had to join the Tsarist army, and Vera and two sisters were taken into the Friends orphanage near Buzuluk for two years until he returned. In the orphanage Vera knew Florence Barrow, the Quaker who managed the institution. In the wake of the famine of 1922, the family made their way mostly on foot back across almost 2,000km to return to their land. Vera's two sisters died of starvation on the journey, and her father died of typhus a few weeks after arriving home. While doing field work for her new assignment in Poland, Florence Barrow found Vera alone in her village and took her to the Horodec outpost to learn spinning and weaving. Vera lived with the staff of the outpost until 1925, and when she went back to her village she was given a loom. In 1936 she was still living in the District, married with three children, and still weaving to earn extra income. [17]

Muriel A. Heagney (1885–1974) Muriel was a trade union and women's rights activist, born into a working class family in Brisbane, Australia. She trained as a teacher, and in WWI worked as the first female clerk in the Defence Department. At the same time she was active in the anti-conscription campaign. She was the General Secretary of the Australian Relief Fund for Stricken Europe from 1921 to 1923 which raised £83,200 for relief projects. Using an honorarium of £100 she received for this work she went to Europe at the end of 1923 to see how the money had been used. She met with the Quakers in London, which led to her being invited in February 1924 to spend some time working with the relief mission in Poland. Muriel was assigned to manage the Women's Industries at the Horodec Outpost, a position which she handed over to Margaret in the fall of 1924. From Poland she continued on for a two month visit to the Soviet Union in 1925 before returning to Australia in the fall. Muriel was a labour activist in Australia for the rest of her life. Equal pay for women was her driving passion which she researched, wrote, and lobbied for, and saw accepted in principle before she died at 89. [25, 26]

Richard R. Taylor (1901–1974) An American Quaker from Baltimore, Richard graduated in engineering before being sent by AFSC to Poland to join the relief work in mid 1923. He stayed in Poland until 1925. In 1924 he had been working at the Horodec Outpost, managing the sawmill. The sawmill was the last remaining element of a Friends project which had helped homeless peasants collect timber from government forests, mill it, and rebuild their homes. About 45,000 cubic metres of timber was moved to rebuild more than 3,000 homes. The project wrapped up in the spring of 1924, and Richard stayed on until the fall to finish processing the last remaining timber. In 1925 he returned to the US where he married three times and had four children. In 1963 his third marriage was to Rebecca Timbres Clark who had been an AFSC volunteer in Poland in 1921. [13]

18 December 1924, Warsaw, Instalment 6

A week later Margaret returns to Warsaw to participate in the regular meetings of the Komitet Pomocy Polskim Kresom Wschodnim, (KPPKW, the Committee for Help to the Polish Eastern Borders), and the Industries Committee, a sub-committee of the KPPKW, where management decisions about the project are made. Interestingly, it appears that the Friends representatives (mainly international staff) hold a 'pre-meeting', before the formal KPPKW meeting with their Polish counterparts. Quakers have a long tradition of conducting meetings on the basis of patient discussion and consensus decision making. This may be a new approach for Margaret who is more of a woman of action, and finds these meetings tedious.

Dear People,

I am afraid the keeping of a diary is becoming more and more spasmodic; all last week I seemed to be preparing for going down to Warsaw and most of this seems to have been spent recovering from coming back.

It was of course only ten days since my last visit, but there were two Committees to attend, and as many things to talk over about the work as if I had not been down for months. The Exhibition had been most successful, - or rather that is incorrect, it was a failure on the whole, but speaking comparatively from our point of view, - for our small stall had sold more than any other in the building, and it was perhaps quite the most unpretentious. Baby's feeders especially were in great demand; they are turned out by the thousand in Powursk, the cross stitch district and have all sorts of fascinating little figures on, - little men, dogs and hens and bees and turkeys. They are real interpretive art; the peasants illustrate all they see, even to bringing in designs with the louse rampant! Jane however unfeelingly put a stop to that; she is evidently no believer in the doctrine 'tout ce qui est dans la nature est dans l'art.'

I went down to Warsaw on Friday night and we had the Industry Committee on Saturday morning. The Committee refused with one accord to consider the Priest's proposal, and if the letter was sent off as arranged it must have reached the gentlemen yesterday; we do not know if it has of course, but we are feeling a little like the lull before the storm; he has had a consultation with the chimney lady anyway today, if that is anything to go by.

On Saturday afternoon we set out to go and hear a lantern lecture given by Wilmer Young to an Orphanage on the work of the Mission in Poland. When we got there we found the whole household busy arranging and decorating for Christmas; the girls (all dressed in black with black pinafores) looked very jolly and happy, and seemed to have plenty of freedom. They just live in the Orphanage and all go to different schools; we saw two studies, the dining room and the kitchen. Having arrived, at two minutes past the time fixed for the lecture, we discovered that the place was lighted by gas, and the lantern we had brought with us could only work with electric light. So with mutual and profuse apologies, there was nothing for it but to look around the building and return home.

On Sunday morning I discovered the existence of an English Church; it is made in a large room of a flat, just the right size for a small number of people to prevent it looking empty, and to accommodate probably as many as are ever likely to turn up, comfortably. The man who took the service adapted himself to the size of the place too, there was a 'hearty' variety of harmonium, and everyone seemed to enjoy the service thoroughly. I certainly did, - as much for the Englishness of it as anything else.

The Chaplain issued a general invitation to everyone to come and practise Xmas hymns in the afternoon, and have tea in their flat afterwards; I should rather have liked to have gone, but had already arranged to go to a concert at the Philharmonic with Jane. There was a ripping Orchestra, and an English singer, Berta Crawford, very Italian in style. She did wonderful things with her voice, and chose mainly operatic things or songs with heaps of trills and cascades of notes, but it was difficult to follow her words in any language. The great thing of the afternoon was Tchaikovsky's Symphonic Pathetique, which they played magnificently. After the concert Jane invited me to tea in a tea shop near, and then we went back to the flat and wrote letters, and had a picnic supper. Muriel Heagney was still staying there but had been writing articles all day, so that she had not come out with us.

Monday was spent, practically the whole day in Committee. Early in the morning I went with Jane to meet Ruth Fry and then departed to find a dentist, and buy cards for Christmas, and then as soon as Ruth Fry had come down to the Office we started a preliminary Committee among the Friends Representatives which continued the whole of the afternoon, until the [KPPKW] Committee proper at five. The preliminary stunt is a very rambling affair, and the other moves a little quicker, but both are the most lifeless kinds I have ever met. You don't feel that any real business is done in Committee or any real decisions made, or that an individual member has any particular contribution to make; circulating minutes (or a full agenda, which is practically equivalent) would answer the purpose equally well. The charming manner of the chairman, and tea and petits fours are the only compensation. I can't help wondering what the busy men on the Polish side think of that way of passing their precious time; - Mr. Grabski's secretary comes, the Minister of Agriculture was there last time, and representatives from other ministries.

Jane suggested my staying on until Tuesday night to hear Ruth Fry speak, but unfortunately we had run short of various cottons wanted for next morning at the distribution, and besides now such a lot of women are coming in, it is rather too heavy for Sophia Wrzeszcz to manage alone; but I was sorry because I should have liked to hear her.

At the station I was astonished to see on arriving the most wonderful edition of an old green horse bus that you ever saw, with a driver's seat on the roof, - otherwise no outside. I suppose it plies between some distant village and the station and that it is a relic of the middle of the last century. It must be a good deal warmer than a furmanka.

The weather is sometimes very cold indeed, - and sometimes ten times colder than that, but on the whole I suppose Poland as well as England has had a mild autumn. Snow has been on the ground for weeks, though there has been only about one fall of snow, some six inches deep, and in the sun it looks simply wonderful, much as I imagine it must do in Switzerland, with yellow and pink lights, and blue shadows, often dazzlingly sparkling. When there is no sun all the colour seems to die out of the earth; sometimes we get up and find a heavy opaque mist of dull grey, the trees covered with frost an inch thick, looking like dead blossom, seem to belong to an unreal world, though they are too substantial to be ghostly.

xx xxx xx

A. Ruth Fry (1878–1962) Ruth was an English Quaker from a large wealthy family in London. As the daughter of a prominent judge she was educated at home with her siblings, several of whom went on to be activists and writers. Ruth began her activism during the Boer War. In 1914 she began 10 years as the general secretary of the Friends War Victims Relief Committee (FRC). In 1919 she was a member of a joint UK-US mission to offer Quaker assistance to the new Polish government, which started the Friends work in Poland. In 1924, aged 47, she was in her final year with FRC when she visited Warsaw to attend regular committee meetings. Ruth had also been chair of the Russian Famine Relief Fund in 1921, and went on to be the secretary of the National Council for the Prevention of War in 1926–27, and treasurer of the London branch of the War Resisters' International in 1936–37. She travelled extensively for the Quakers during and after World War One and was again a pacifist during World War Two. [14]

Wladyslaw D. Grabski (1874–1938) An economist, historian and politician, Grabski was born into the Polish aristocracy under the Russian

Empire. He graduated from the Sorbonne in Paris and returned to Poland to found an Agricultural Society in his home district, which attracted the support of many peasants. He was imprisoned by the Tsarist authorities as an activist, and after his release in 1905 he was elected to the Russian Imperial Duma. During World War One he joined the Polish National Committee which sided with Russia and the Entente. He was prime minister for one month in 1920. In 1922 he took over the direction of the Polish-American Children's Relief Committee (PAKPD), which had responsibility for distribution and administration of children's relief in Poland, and had been the local partner of the American Relief Administration (ARA). In 1923 he was appointed prime minister a second time and was still in office in 1924 when he was invited by the Friends to be a member of the Advisory Committee overseeing the work of their Kolpin Orphanage and Agricultural School. As Prime Minister he created the Bank of Poland, and a new zloty currency, and temporarily halted the hyperinflation which had the Friends carrying suitcases of currency to fund the Women's Industries. After resigning as prime minister in 1925 he was rector of the Warsaw Agricultural University for the rest of his life. [4, 18, 27]

21 December 1924, Horodec

This letter also continues after Margaret's return to Horodec, with more discussion about the question of the house leases, and a round of visits to local power brokers.

Today there is thaw, and the place is a disgusting mess of half melted snow; the creatures to rejoice are the ducks and geese, and they are signifying their approval very audibly; the ducks are wriggling their bills down into the mud for worms, and the geese are pretending to have a bath in the three inch deep puddle round the door step. I am feeling very sad, because unless we have a sudden change, gone is my last hope of driving down from Brest to Kolpin by sleigh, which I should simply have adored to do. There will be chances enough later of driving in a sleigh, but none that could ever have been so fitting a Christmas Eve, could it?

It is funny to see the zeal which we are apparently putting into making local contacts; as a matter of fact, except for our proposal to the Vojt, we are probably doing nothing different from what would have been done in the ordinary course of affairs, but every move takes on a new significance. We have paid a friendly visit to the school master and mistress, and offered them some woolly caps left over from the mission for Christmas celebrations among their children; we are presenting as a Christmas box to the station master and director of transport a wonderful beetroot rug (each with emerald green and orange stripes!); we are selling spare furmanka parts and presenting an old tarpaulin which had already been lent to him to the estate owner here, - the one who summoned us the other day for some matter connected with oats and hay.

The one deliberate move we have made is to offer the present distribution room to the police if they can come to terms with our landlord; we sent a note to the Vojt asking him if we would come and see us this time, so that we could talk over the matter more quietly as we had not yet broached the subject to our landlord; he replied that he would come on Saturday, and behold on Saturday morning [Haim-Nisl Vinograd] the distribution house Jew arrives saying that he had heard from someone at the Gmina that we wanted to let his house to the Police, - a nice way of treating confidential communication, don't you think? The Vojt has done nothing but prejudice his own cause by tackling the affair like that, and when I asked him if he knew that the landlord had already been informed by some one at the Gmina he shrugged his shoulders. If however by offering a higher rent than we are paying he can come to terms with the man we shall move the loom and spinning wheels to the room that was formerly the saw mill office in the house where we sleep, and have the distributions there too.

I am succumbing to the temptation to furnish my room with my own things while I am here, and by degrees hope to collect rugs, bed-cover and cushion covers, with orange for the chief tone and strips and things in blues and brown and crimson. One cushion cover is already in the cupboard, but not yet appropriated, the rug I like best of any has already been made several times, but the great excitement will be a bedspread in flax and wool something after the same design as the rug, - a totally new experiment! My room will be perfectly wonderful by the time it is finished; a week or two ago I made pictures for the household out of magazine covers and cardboard, and now I am having shelves put in an old wardrobe in the office; it is very rickety but a very nice grained wood, walnut I think, and will lend the new room an air of great distinction, I feel sure.

Now that the weather is cold, and more and more women come in for the distribution, the scene becomes increasingly comic; in spite of the fact that one woman will bring in work for six, and that we try to take the women from the more distant villages in the morning, they seem to have no idea of arranging the time among themselves, and they arrive soon after daylight and wait until evening; we give them numbers of that they will come in in turn, but they jam themselves, fifty or more into the porch and try to invade the room every time the door opens; they have to be restrained by main force, but once they are in it is impossible to get them out. The most effective way is to give them three minutes to clear out again under penalty of having no more work that day, and then they jam and push and shove and mostly make their way out. They never seem to lose their tempers and an English crowd would if they shoved like that, they seem just like a herd of cows crowding along a narrow lane, and take it just as naturally. Some of them are frightfully funny, when they come in; they talk very loudly very quickly, without a single pause, and go on and on till Sophia Wrzeszcz and I nearly have hysterics; others grumble at the money they get, some are pleased, and others, dignified and capable, take the whole matter with the serious air of people who do good work and know it.

At Muriel Heagney's last distribution one old woman came in, thrust some bad work at her and said, "There! I know it's bad, you can scold me if you like, you needn't pay me anything, but I hadn't time to do it better; I am a beggar and I am far too busy begging really to do any work, and I shan't take any more in the future." She had also brought along with her a whole lot of work that had been outstanding for months; the women had been afraid to bring it back themselves, lest they should be scolded, but she said that she already had everything possible said to her in her life, that she was too thick skinned to mind! So far from scolding her, I believe they offered her a premium to collect the rest, but she has disappeared again.

A happy new year to you all. Margaret.

xx xxx xx

Haim-Nisl Vinograd and Abraham Vinograd (1908–1944?) Haim-Nisl was a Jewish store owner and trader in Horodec who was involved with the local lumber business. Before the war he would leave home for weeks at a time, roaming the forests and bringing boatloads of timber along the Dnieper-Bug Canal. When the Russians retreat began in 1915 Haim-Nisl, like many of the Jewish population, stayed behind, hoping that the Germans would provide a more liberal administration than the Russians had done. Like everyone else in his community, he took up farming after the peasants left to feed his family. He lost his house during the war but rebuilt after the fighting finished. When the Friends opened their outpost in Horodec in 1921 Haim-Nisl rented them part of his new house for office and living space, while he and his family lived in the rest of the house. Haim-Nisl spoke mainly Yiddish, but could understand the German which many of the Friends volunteers knew, including Margaret. Haim's son, Abraham was 17 in 1925 and still at school. Abraham went on to become a corporal in the Polish Army, spoke good Polish and read Polish literature. After the Nazis took Horodec in 1941, Abraham died fighting with the Partisans, while the rest of the family were killed in the Holocaust in 1942 or 43. [1]

4 January 1925, Stradetz

Margaret spends Christmas 1924 visiting another Friend's project, the Kolpin Agricultural School and Orphanage. The Quakers wanted to leave some kind of permanent institution behind when they left Poland, and so they decided to set up an agricultural school and orphanage with the particular aim of helping landowning youth, who were orphaned by the war, get the training they needed to make use of the land they had inherited.

In August 1923 a 110 hectare (280 acres) estate near Stradetz, which had been confiscated from an absentee Russian owner, was leased to the Friends by the Polish government for 12 years. It was expected that once the school was up and running it would be turned over to the Ministry of Agriculture. The institution formally opened and the first students started in October 1924. In 1924–25 there were about 25 older boys studying agriculture and 20 younger orphans being taken care of. [4, 11]

When Margaret gets back to Horodec she hosts a Christmas party for the young girls who work on the project looms. (The Priest's house has a damaged, but had a workable wind-up gramophone.) The Belarusian peasant women are demanding increasing work through the project, and the current staff are having trouble keeping up on their side. Margaret finds that she doesn't know how to motivate her Polish colleagues to keep up with her punishing pace, and admits that she is having trouble learning Polish and communicating.

Dear People,

A very happy new year to you all. Christmas already seems some months ago. It came very suddenly, almost unexpectedly; I couldn't realise at all that it was upon us, because there were so few preparations to make I suppose; - no whispered consultations as to 'what are you going to get for so-and-so?' or mysterious excursions to some hiding place in response to the invitation to 'come and see what I've got for Mother'. But on Tuesday we met the postman with heaps of letters and packages, and explored the resources of the village store to get ingredients for a cake Miss Stankiewicz intended to make while I was away, and when on Wednesday morning, there were Christmas trees that the police had cut down and stuck on the coal truck where they were riding behind the engine I began to believe in it a little.

I had a long wait of over four hours in Brest (Brzesc-Litewski as it is really called) before Jane and Mr. [Ladislas] Skoraczewski (the disconsolate husband who played bridge with us in Warsaw) arrived, so I set out to explore the town. It was difficult to know which direction to try, so I looked out the most interesting buildings from the high railway bridge, and struck out in the direction of the Russian Church; it was the kind of building you see in pictures, with rounded arches and gilded towers with dark green inverted-turnip shaped tops, and fascinated me by its unfamiliarity. The only other building of any size that I could see was also a church, big whitewashed and uninteresting. The rest of the town was absolutely nothing to look at; a great many of the houses were just temporary buildings, and all of it showed signs of hasty post war construction. On the other hand nothing indicated that Brzesc ever had been in any way a grand ville. I supposed it owes its importance to the splendid natural position for defence that it occupies on the river.

We passed the fortress where the treaty was signed, but it was hidden by the trees. It was a long drive, nearly three hours, to Kolpin, over the most desolate countryside imaginable; if life in the trenches can be more horrible in one place than in the other, it must have been over these battlefields, - dead flat colourless frozen marshes. The last part of our drive was finished in the dark. Jane and I were shown up into the room we were to share together, and had barely finished tidying when we were called down to go to the children's supper.

There were about forty of them I should think, very much scrubbed for the occasion, looking very 'institution-y' crowded into a small bare room with wooden walls and floors, having supper of soup, raw herrings and potatoes; we watched them eat for a little while and then retreated, not knowing quite what to do there, but when we were fetched to the bigger boys, we saw the whole of the ceremony. Some of them received us with the politest bows, - which seemed so incongruous with their general rather plough boy appearance, and took us into their dining room which was much bigger (we learnt afterwards that the two 'nest-fulls' are only sharing one room until the second house is finished) and in the corner of which was a wonderful Christmas tree, practically all the decorations for which they had made themselves. It is the custom, before the Christmas Eve dinner to break a piece of wafer on which is stamped a picture of the crèche, at least with your neighbour if not with everyone in the room, and to wish them a happy Xmas. The boys passed some on to their neighbours but Miss [Jadwiga] Bialowieska, and the house mothers and the Director went practically all the way round. Then the Director made a speech to the boys while their soup got cold, and at the end they rose with one accord like clockwork and said 'thank you, sir!' sat down again all together and fell to.

We went through the wafer ceremony again before our own supper, which was also the traditional fish supper, but somewhat more elaborate than the children's. We had soup with a fish flavour, the same salt raw herrings, but other cooked fish as well, with potatoes and cold pickled sauerkraut, and a pudding of cold cooked poppy seed with biscuits to decorate it. Just at the end we heard a noise at the door, and in from the garden trooped all the children, the first one holding a large illuminated paper lantern, and began to sing carols; the lantern turned round and round and sheep and other figures seemed to be moving inside; the children gazed fascinatedly at it as they sang, and so far from being self conscious, seemed to have lost themselves entirely in the greatness of the occasion; after the lantern came a illuminated star which the small boy who held it kept on turning; they sang more carols, and at the end presented the lantern to Erling (that is his Christian name really but the surname [Kjekstad] is too much of a strain to spell; likewise henceforth I think I shall refer to Miss Bialowieska as 'Jadwiga', and Mr. Skoraczewski as 'Skora') Inside was a minute crèche, doll and all in the cradle, that the children had made; it was a perfect work of art. Jadwiga received the star, and two string bags from two little girls who explained that that was the first work they had made.

Then they all went in to the Christmas tree; a huge tree, beautifully decorated with heaps and heaps of parcels lying underneath; the light from the candles lit up the whole room and the children were spell bound. The tiniest boy, a fair, fragile, typical waif, moved about the whole evening in a kind of ecstatic dream; as luck would have it his was practically the last parcel to be given out, but it wasn't until he had been watching more than half an hour that he seemed to bother about what was coming to him; the whole scene was too wonderful. First there were more carols round the tree everyone joining hands in two rings; all the people who worked anywhere about the place were there too, and the children seemed to enjoy their getting a parcel just as much as their own. The older boys had ties and handkerchiefs, and the younger children parcels of toys. The visitors had presents too, I had a Jack in the box which was a great success, and a fascinating small wooden doll which a jointed neck and a demure expression, which I christened Drusilla Jane.

After the presents came nuts and fruit and cakes, a little more singing and then bed for the children. They thanked everyone and said goodnight, all the boys with beautiful little bows and the girls with curtsies. One little girl curtsied, then suddenly turned her back to us with a finger to her brow and stood motionless for a moment; we had just time to wonder what was happening when she turned round and curtsied again with a prettily spoken English 'Goodnight'. Wasn't that charming of her?

We played bridge until fairly late, and lay long in bed the next morning. I had kept my home letters, and my parcel and sat up and read them in bed joining the party in Mother's room in imagination, and quite probably at the wrong hour!! There was nothing really Christmassy about the whole day until we joined the children again in the evening, except that we ate a great many nice things which seems to be an indispensible part of celebrating in every country; it was very pleasant but nobody seemed to have the "Aye, therefor be merry, set sorrow aside" feeling, except the kiddies whose mouth organs, trumpets, etc. were going incessantly. After breakfast we wandered round the place; there are four or five buildings beside the main one where the heads live, two cottages called nests for the orphans and one or two buildings for the elder boys studying agriculture. Everything is of the barest and roughest, and at present the accommodation is rather crowded, but of course the whole place is very much in its infancy.

The children do all their own orderly work share in the farm, looking after the animals etc. help with the cooking as well as going to their school. I think that it is a ripping system provided they really have free time as well and a real chance of play and leisure. They probably find it heavenly compared with their past experiences. There is a small girl there called Anna, who looks a though she might be five and small at that, but they say she is nine a least; she has been alone for some years, I don't know quite how long, but three years ago she was being hired out to earn her living keeping pigs in a field; she walked 20 km along, without boots to get to the place from which she was to be brought to Kolpin. When you look at the tiny mite it seems absolutely incredible.

Then we went down to the Bug (pronounced boog as they will tell you in [Council for International Service] C.I.S. leaflets, lest your tender susceptibilities be injured) which flows at the bottom of the garden and took photographs on the ice, and watched Erling and other people struggle with arrangements they were trying to make to produce electricity for the cinema he has just bought; they couldn't get it to go satisfactorily, so had to wait till Boxing Day when one of the saw mill mechanics came to work the tractor.

In the evening we were invited to the children's own Christmas tree in the school room; they had evidently been told how to play hosts, and they did it beautifully; saw that we were never standing for more than a second, - if we moved, our chairs were brought after us; insisted with

Jane Pontefract, Margaret, and Ladislas Skoraczewski, Christmas Day 1924. *On the frozen Bug River during a Christmas visit to the Friends' agricultural school and orphanage at Koplin. The school was meant to be the Friends' legacy project in Poland, but it was closed within three years due to lack of funds.*

polite ceremony on our having some of everyone's sweets, looked after the candles on the trees; and saw that the little ones didn't get in front of us; their teacher must have been proud of them. I liked the tone very much – they move freely, are not the least shy or afraid of anyone, enjoy themselves with much natural noise but without being rough or rowdy. I accumulated a lot of ideas on an orphanage and if any of you know someone who want to endow quite a small one, I beg to apply for the job of running it!

More bridge, well into the early morning this time, and breakfast in bed in consequence; Jane and I read most of the time, while the men folk all concentrated on the cinema which was ready to work by the evening. The films were not good but the lantern is, and there seem some possibilities in having one.

Of course the boys loved it, but the principal things that aroused them to articulate mirth was the sight of anyone embracing and a ghastly incident where little sunshine shakes his dead mummy for about five minutes to try and wake her.

Jane came back to Horodec for the weekend before going on to Powursk for her distribution, and returned here on Thursday morning in time for our loom girl's party. On her way back, the expected happened, and while she was in Zablochy station about one in the morning, a train bandit got in and seized her fur coat and rucksack. She dashed after him and got to the door in time to make him drop the coat, and yelled for the police who gave chase. She thinks if she had followed him herself she could have caught him, but he got down away from the platform, nobody would have seen and she couldn't risk the train going on without her. As it was he got away. She went to notify the police in Brzes´c´ when the train got there, and the man there remarked that she shouldn't have been sleeping. Considering that it was her third night running in the train that was rather adding insult to injury and she let him know what she thought of the inefficient way they guard trains. Then he went on to question her about her father and mother's Christian names and their place of birth, her religion, and everything under the sun but not the contents of the rucksack. Luckily she had the bulk of the money on her person, and nothing in the rucksack was frightfully valuable.

We held our loom party in the old office; on Wednesday we asked Potonia to get some green for decorations, and lo and behold he returned with a large Xmas tree. So we felt we must rise to the occasion, and after work on Wednesday set out to make decorations, - paper chains, roses, stars, little baskets, figures cut out and pasted on cardboard, etc. One of the embroidery girls took some home for her sister to do and arrived back the next morning with a simply perfect cotton wool Santa Claus, a lovely flying swan and various other things.

When we added gingerbreads in silver paper, crackers and candles the tree looked perfectly thrilling and not the least bare. We tied up soap and scent and handkerchiefs, brooches and little books, combs and mirrors in twelve parcels, and put those in two boxes for the girls to fish for with a line and a bent pin. At seven they all arrived, very much in their best, with curled hair and with hair ribbons. Vera, the girl who lives in the house sports a pink taffeta with frills!

I did enjoy the party; they are so game for anything. We played musical chairs, then they sang carols to us, pulled crackers, fished for their presents, and then danced. They dance mostly waltzes, very vigorously, polkas, and a thing called the pas d'Espagne and a very fast Polish dance whose name I have forgotten. Helena, a girl who does embroidery, waltzes rippingly, I loved dancing with her.

From quite early on we had half the village children peering in at the windows and when we opened the door to cool the room, there they were crowding into the passage way outside to get a glimpse of the tree; so we suddenly hauled them in made them play musical bumps there and then just as they were, about thirty of them with a prize of chocolate for those ones who kept in the longest; curiosity here is not a sin, it is a question of natural interest, and all sorts of people wandered into the house and looked in at the door; it was rather fun hauling the children in even though we had to boot them out again immediately. Refreshments consisting of bread and butter and jam, tea, and chocolate biscuits provided by Sophia Wrzeszcz, with a final dance or two completed the evening. They nearly all kiss one's hand on saying good night which I think is a perfectly awful plan, and causes me the most acute discomfort.

They enjoyed it quite as much as we did, and enquired early of Miss Stankiewicz the next day if we were pleased with the way they had behaved, just like kids instead of grown up girls. We are hoping to have them in again, - the club plan has never got started, life has been so full, but we are all feeling keener on it and now may manage to do something about it.

Work grows daily more and more; heaps and heaps of women coming into the distributions, which have lasted this week from nine till eight thirty and from ten thirty to ten at night, and in consequence there is proportionately more cutting out, more laundry to check and sort, more work to price. I very much hope that we are going to have a fourth worker; Sophia Wrzeszcz's cousin [Miss Givoult] is coming up for a month and if we find she fits in and is a great help we shall keep her. Miss Stankiewicz nearly departed for good this week; she was very injured at being left here for Christmas and said that if we wouldn't give her a holiday next week, she would go for good. I did not say her nay; it is impossible to let her go willingly before Sophia Wrzeszcz's cousin comes, because however much we wanted to do her work as well as our own it is a practical impossibility; but she changed her mind. I don't know whether to be glad or sorry; she is most methodical and conscientious but her ineffable resignation is irritating to the last degree, and I'm not sure that she will ever be really happy here, she has absolutely no resources for her spare time, except reading, and she has few books. Apparently, according to her cousin who Mrs. Henoch knows, she always cultivates the martyr stunt and it doesn't really mean she is unhappy, so in time I shall doubtless cease to worry about her. I have already given up active methods of trying entertainment. I took her for a walk and her chilblains hurt her but she sacrificed herself in silence till nearly the end; I taught her all the Patiences [solitaire] and games for two that I knew one evening, and Jane and I played cards, most gentle ones, with her the whole of another, and were already feeling our wings sprouting, when she announced that she didn't think she would ever get as far as to learn bridge; cards bored her thoroughly, and she never played except with her little niece (and to oblige us I suppose).

At meals we have already given up having a permanent common conversation which is perhaps a pity, but so much less effort; she and Sophia Wrzeszcz (or rather mainly Sophia Wrzeszcz) talk Polish, and Sophia Wrzeszcz, and I English; any specially interesting tit bit being translated to one or the other, because we two found it absolutely impossible to draw her in or interest her when we kept it up in French. Miss Givoult talks a little French and no English so I shall be forced at last to learn some Polish when she comes I suppose. I am ashamed to think how little I have learnt, but not sufficiently to make me sit down and work at the wretched tongue.

Everybody else's Christmas in these parts happens next week; - Russian calendar! I got quite a shock though when Miss Stankiewicz announced that the cook did not want to go home next week but she would like to go for New Years day! on Wednesday week.

In the middle of writing this I had a visit from [AbrahamVinograd], the son of the distribution house Jew and he said that the Vojt had not even communicated with his Father. Really they are extraordinary people! Much love from Margaret

xx xxx xx

Jacob 'Yashka' Gryn (1913–??) Yashka was born in the Horodec District on a small holding of about two hectares. When he was still an infant, he was evacuated with his family of six deep into Russia in 1915 as far as the Kirghiz Steppes. Along the way he lost his parents and grandmother, and after eight years came back with two teenaged brothers. After his brother got work with the Horodec mission he was brought to the outpost, where he was put in charge of cleaning the boots and other errands. His brother was drafted by the Polish army, and he was left alone with the Friends. Despite his hard life, he was a cheerful and helpful boy. When the Kolpin Agricultural School was set up in 1924 he was included in the first class. The Polish government had committed to land reform that would give children like Yashka title to their parents land. The Friends hoped that with training in modern agricultural technology these orphans would make their land productive and have a secure future. [4]

Erling Kjekstad (1895–??) Erling was a Norwegian Quaker who was left by his unmarried parents to grow up in an orphanage. As a teenager he was sent to Denmark to learn to be a gardener, and there was influenced by the religious beliefs of the nursery owners who were followers of the famous Danish thinker, N.F.S. Grundtvig. Grundtvig advocated a Christian faith expressed through living and deeds. In 1916, when he was 21 he spent six months in England working at a nursery in East Grinstead, Sussex, and was strongly inclined towards pacifism by his encounters with the wounded from France. In 1921 he went to the Quakers' Fircroft

College of Adult Education in Birmingham and that December volunteered to work with the Quakers. From 1922 he worked with the Friends in Poland for about five years. In 1923 he supervised the timber hauling project from Horodec, and then from 1924 to 1927 he was the Quaker representative and Controller at the Kolpin Agricultural School and Orphanage. On his return to Norway he was an active Quaker in Oslo, and kept in touch with English Quakers, visiting the Quaker's Woodbrooke College in Birmingham in 1929. [28]

15 January 1925, Horodec

By January Margaret is settling into life in a small rural town, but she continues to have communication problems. A new staff member, Miss Golonowska, arrives to help out, but she doesn't speak English or French.

Dear People,

I am afraid this won't be an awfully long instalment this time, as the typewriter has bust, and the little jigger that holds the ribbon gets stuck every two letters or so, and at the moment I'm attempting typing without any ribbon at all, which leaves me quite in the dark as to what I have said. Moreover, history is given to repeating itself, even in the lives of the greatest, and I suppose the stock of new events must gradually dwindle.

My chief occupations of the last week or two have been trying to invent new jumper patterns, experimenting with new kinds of woven bedspreads; both achievements made me swell with pride, which was shortly to meet its just punishment. Inspired by ideas about my own room I wanted to produce a bedcover that would make my name go blessed by the whole posterity of "bed-sitting-roomers", - something that would look part of the room and match the rug on the floor, and have cushions to hold the pillows and bolster, that would match. The history is too long to unfold piecemeal, but suffice it that I took our gentle Miss Stankiewicz aside and pointed out to her with the real rug on a real bed, just exactly where the big band of design had to come; was also rash enough to tell her how much margin to leave to hang down; the first one turned out most successfully; then some days later, it was suggested that we already had some definite measurements asked for by either London or America, - I forget which, - and I passed these on to the dear lady. Then a few days ago, thinking I would pay a visit to the loom room, I discovered to my horror that the dear intelligent soul, having been given a length of the whole bedspread, - and having once been told what edge to leave, when it came to shorten the whole, cut the middle out, on the grim principle of "let us obey orders or die!". So there is still plenty of edge, - all the edge asked for, - but instead of hanging down the sides, it lies neatly and flatly on top of the bed. My luck with jumpers was almost worse; there the cutting lady after the most careful explanations, just through sheer carelessness, or love of the unusual, cut all the front openings down the back, for a change. The other new venture is a night dress, and I'm certain they'll sew up the bottom of those.

I have also been busy working out the exact amount of embroidery that can be expected from so many skeins of cotton, so that we can really pounce on offenders with some accuracy; you feel you need the support of something in the way of figures, when they pour out torrents of protestations. They are awfully funny always deny having taken cotton, but when you say they won't get any more work or money till they bring it back, some offer to take as much work as you will give them and work it with the cotton they have just sworn they haven't got; others if they don't live too far away go off and return with it in an hour or two, giving for their excuse, if questioned "My mother didn't give it me all", or "The children must have hidden it". One lady who hadn't been found out, had been told to do a darning stitch, which takes far less cotton than the Drohiczyn stitch, but she preferred doing that and brought back a whole lot of work in red, white and blue, - a most wonderful combination; when we asked her about it she said she happened to have the blue and white at home!

We have got a new helper, a Miss Golonowska, who has come for a month on trial. Sophia Wrzeszcz's cousin couldn't come and I felt we could very well do with another person so Jane is letting us have one to try. She seems very pleasant; is 23, knows very very little English, and no other language except Polish and some Chinese, I believe, - which isn't particularly helpful. One point in her favour is that she is said to be very keen on dancing, - especially of the plastic variety.

The Priest is still here, although he no longer officiates in church; the atmosphere [illegible] is calm on the whole, though he has again refused to let us fix our stove in Miss Heagney's old room. The Vojt has taken no notice of our offer to hand over our room so we are putting up another loom there and are using the old office for a distribution room.

We are just doing for ourselves for ever, by sending in a bill to the Commandant for the rug which he obviously wanted to have as a bribe.

We had an excitement nearer home at the beginning of the week; an old peasant woman who had just sold her land was robbed and hanged on the road between here and Antopol. I felt quite glad that Miss Golonowska brought the money with her this time instead of having to fetch it from the post. Wasn't it a brutal thing to do?

Tymie grows and is almost a cat; he is very clumsy, and not in the least intelligent, but he tries to make up for both by demonstrative affection. He rubs himself against my feet if he can't go at anything else, and tries it on with my Wellington boots, even if I am in the room, and is most terribly injured that my second pair of legs don't seem as stable as my first. The other morning I called him at breakfast to come and eat a saucerful of milk which I had placed beside my chair; he always comes when he is called, - and follows me out of doors like a dog; well he came now, purring with gratification, and gazing at me with a look of passionate devotion on his upturned face, walked slowly, heavily and deliberately, right into the saucer of milk!

I really cannot bear this type writer any more; someone is trying to borrow a screw driver for us from a man he once heard had one, - I only hope it will materialize. And I will write a longer letter next time; I'll also enclose [a poem] the results of a spasm just after Christmas which may amuse you to see; it wasn't written for readers of the journal, because you have heard it all before, - but the form thereof will be new to you. If anyone doesn't get an answer to a letter, they may conclude that theirs never reached me; - I know two and probably three have got lost lately, - it is beastly not feeling certain of getting them. Today letters are delayed by the wheels having come off the furmanka of the man what fetches them; the rescue party has set out but we have been told we cannot expect letters until the morning.

Much love to all, Margaret.

31 January 1925, Horodec

After only a few months on the job, but with plenty of time to think about the workings of the project, Margaret begins to question the economics of the industry. She can see the weakness of a project that purports to take advantage of a peasant women's 'spare time' and she questions whether the project can generate enough income for the peasant women through a home-based craft industry. And she recognises that she is somehow stuck in the middle. On the one hand she is responsible for producing marketable products which will sell in the English market. On the other hand, the project wants to employ disadvantaged refugees who have trouble relating to the product specifications Margaret thinks are important. She is frustrated that she isn't communicating effectively, but she can't think of how to get her messages across. But she has some entertaining encounters too, including a marriage proposal.

Dear People,

The neighbourhood was scoured for a screwdriver; but none was forthcoming. So we had one bought and sent from Warsaw and Mr Lance came round to tackle the typewriter. Like the dog that died however, it was the screw driver that got twisted and the machine is still stubbornly unworkable. Hence this pencil and carbon-paper.

I suppose my most starling piece of news since last time is that I have had a proposal to become engaged to a Pole! Don't get excited; it wasn't a proposal to get married, only to get engaged, - and even that wasn't allowed to get very far! The man who owns the house where we have our distribution at Drohiczyn used to be a motor mechanic in America, many years ago and he now wants to return. It is very difficult to get a passport, and so taking me for American – as everyone here does – he asked Sophia Wrzeszcz to ask me when I go back, to take him with me as my fiancé. He said "Of course I should not expect her to keep to it when she got there,

- she could look out for something better." But his wife who either considered me dangerous as a rival, - or thought his charms were such that I should never agree to let him go again rejoiced wholeheartedly on hearing I was English and therefore unable to accept the offer!

We have completed several bits of rearranging to our great satisfaction this last week or two – but I doubt if they will make very thrilling telling. Two new looms are up in the old distribution room and the apparatus for making the warp has come up here to the office. Our linen cupboard has been moved there too, scrubbed, and beautifully arranged with different shelves for cut and uncut linen - Warsaw and local varieties. The office is fitted up now as a proper work room for the cutting women and the two girls who do finishing and preparing work and our living room in the Priest's house is kept for sorting and pricing the finished weavings and embroidery. It's a vastly better arrangement and is working excellently.

Then the servants quarters have been whitewashed and spring cleaned and we fitted up Miss Heagney's room for Miss Stankiewicz while she was away, stuffed the cracks of the door with flax and nailed it up with an old blanket, had a new rug made for the floor to match the bedspread and an oil stove and a double window put in, and Sophia Wrzeszcz made white sprigged muslin curtains out of an old frock of hers. Unfortunately I'd forgotten to tell Miss Stankiewicz we were going to move her. I had told her that she would have that room eventually when our third helper arrived, when she first came, but she evidently thought I'd forgotten, and took it very badly; wept the whole day of her return, and in the evening (we had been at the distribution) demanded that Sophia Wrzeszcz and Miss Golonowska should go on sharing a room and that she should return to her old one. I didn't know what to do; I shouldn't have moved her without being convinced it was be far the best arrangement all round. But it's rather dreadful being confronted by a weeping female who swears you are ruining her health and comfort forever. But remembering more than one instance when the lady had naively let out she preferred something she objected to in the first instance and knowing the room to be more comfortable than her old and just as warm, I said that the arrangement had been carefully considered and couldn't be altered; and all seems to be well. I've never met anyone before who made such a tremendous fuss about everything, swearing she would rather die than submit, and then give in completely and utterly apparently forgetting all about her first objections. She has already enlarged on the beauty of the new rug! Altogether the lady worries me not a little and no effort to make her fit in seems to be successful.

While she was away we had a most sociable time – Sophia Wrzeszcz has got a job promised her as Secretary to the Polish Consul in Washington. What [the] Industries will do without her, I can't think, but I am awfully glad for her sake. It has been one of her ambitions for ages, and she ought to have wider experience than she is getting here. Well, she is to start in a month or two, and is busy making her trousseau, so we evolved the brilliant idea of having sewing parties. We celebrated the first one on Saturday afternoon a fortnight ago by collecting three wicker chairs in my room specially tidied up for the occasion, and having tea brought over with dates and figs and oranges that had been sent from Warsaw - and sewed and read 'When We Were Very Young' aloud. It was most cosy and jolly and a change from our usual ways, - we don't generally have tea at all and never visit one another's rooms. But we have had several other séances since. I was very bucked when Sophia Wrzeszcz asked if she might carry out some plans to improve her room the other day and I said I wished she would, I've always wanted her to. She replied "Well before, I was always so tired I never wanted to do anything but lie on my bed or go to bed, but now that I sit in it and write and sew, I should like to do something." I consider that an unsolicited testimonial and give it to you with great pride, especially as I've rather been afraid that I haven't lightened her work as much as I hoped in the beginning. Now since Tuesday there are four of us in full strength things ought to run still more smoothly.

Miss Golonowska is a dear. Very shy but very friendly. Her English is dreadfully minus and becomes absolutely nil through sheer panic when it comes to an instruction of any kind; but on general matters we manage to say quite a lot. I don't know what she is going to be like from the work point of view. She isn't very quick or very intelligent. I am beginning to believe everything that has been said of Poles (when I've instanced Sophia Wrzeszcz I've always been told, "Oh Miss Wrzeszcz is an exception."). I ask you can you do more than mark in pencil exactly where you want thread drawn? And you get them returned drawn in entirely different spots. If you think you've achieved repetition of a particular scarf by shewing the original you find you haven't, so you ask Sophia Wrzeszcz to interpret with instructions, - still nothing is done. You select the wool and stripes and put it in a heap, and behold it is given to be used on a different loom entirely.

I am still struggling with the cutting women. As in spite of all instructions they cannot cut from a paper pattern, I cut out dresses one morning myself and gave them each linen half just as it was to copy. And still they cut the front like the back. The worst offender is under threat of dismissal, - but she is a war widow with two small boys. It's a hateful combination being responsible for turning out decent work and for supporting or taking away the livelihood of the people at this end.

I'm glad this isn't a concern being run for private profit and that I wasn't born a businessman. I know I should fall into all their very worst sins. As it is I spend my days divided between getting the utmost out of the people who work. I was almost going to say for the least money, but as prices are fixed I suppose that is all that prevents me altering that end of it; and sudden decrees as to a Saturday half holiday for the laundress and cutting people who represent our casual labour! To say nothing of very grave doubts about the economics of home industries in general. I wish I knew something about that. Our women can't possibly earn a living wage embroidering – the answer is 'they aren't meant to', - it's supposed to be an extra. But I can't help feeling it's an unsound system and if it wasn't for the other side of keeping the work alive I don't think I should be in agreement with it.

Just before our sewing craze started I had begun to be awfully interested in the evolution of designs here which have evidently grown from the simple diamond form, with probably later introduction of vertical lines and squares. The beginnings are quite easy to work out, but I expect I shall get stuck when it gets to the more complicated ones. I didn't start with any idea of having the growth of it all, I thought I'd just collect some of the designs for future use, and after I'd analyzed a few, saw where they started and got bitten with the passion for research! If I really get it decently worked out I'll circulate a special illustrated edition for those interested, on request. Unfortunately I haven't brought my paints with me, and pen and ink is far less interesting. The colour changes the whole character of the design very often.

No climax or even finale has arrived with regard the Priest. He is still here. Ignores us face to face but borrows everything from the furmanka and gramophone to carbon paper; his successor officiates in the Church here, but I don't think this one goes to his new Parish.

The Commandant has paid up manfully!

Nothing has been heard of Jane Pontefract's rucksack. The Bandits have visited Holoby - the Priest this time whom they had previously warned. I should be terrified of receiving a warning if I were Jane.

We had another Dance for the loom girls. I forget if I told you. It wasn't of course as thrilling as our New Year's party, but I think they enjoyed it very much the same. We taught them – or tried to – one-step and fox trot, because except for one or two who do fancy dances, rather in the style of the Velita, the majority only polka or a very violent waltze.

I must stop now and wrestle with accounts. They are the bane of my life. A month runs into pages and pages with heaps of different columns and cross tables. About 80 zl. was missing after one visit to Drohiczyn, at the beginning of January and I haven't tracked it down yet; I'm afraid it's been stolen, but it is difficult to know by whom.

Best love to all, Margaret

3 March 1925, Warsaw

In February Margaret returns to Warsaw for Committee meetings and meets Florence Barrow who was one of the founding members of the Friends' Polish work. Margaret takes on some 'home decorating' to try and make their otherwise plain accommodations more comfortable.

Dear People,

At last we have the pleasure of welcoming our friend the typewriter back to the bosom of our family; he has been to be cleaned, at least that is what they said they were going to do with him, though the old familiar layers of dust that wrap round those parts of his internals that are visible, seem to keep their ancient places. However, the proof of the pudding...

Since I last wrote I have been down to Warsaw again for Committees. The day before I started, there having been a muddle about the money, Mrs. Henoch's nephew came up to bring us some, and to travel back with me. He was a priceless individual who never stopped talking from the moment he arrived until we parted at the door of the Zlota flat the next morning in Warsaw. We were all very busy,... I was vainly trying to balance accounts and pack the kit bags for Warsaw, and if it hadn't been that Miss Golonowska was going into Antopol in the afternoon, and we suggested that he might like to go with her, I don't think I should ever have got away at all. He was educated at Brighton College and played football against the girls at Roedean; when the war broke out he joined the Guards, TME regiment, and got attached to the British Mission afterwards. He gave the most thrilling account of their holding up the Bolsheviks with an armoured train on the line just near here, and seems to have been in every exciting episode that ever happened. He and his men were the last people to dash across the great bridge across the Vistula the second before they blew it up. It is a huge thing, very wide and very long, and all the middle part is of course new; but Mr. Giszitski says that it was repaired in two weeks by the Germans who were chasing the Russians at that point, - a terrific feat which was only possible because they had reckoned on the bridge being destroyed, and they had brought along duplicate girders etc. with standardised screws. All sorts of anecdotes about the traditions of the Guards he related but it would take too long to try and pass them on. Luckily he didn't talk to me all night; after Brzes´c´ I got half a side on which I curled up and shut my eyes firmly, but two of the other men proved to be acquaintances, and another to have mutual friends, so that at intervals he continued all night long. Considering he had travelled the whole of the previous night, and had not closed an eye all day, I was filled with wonder and admiration.

The great excitement about the Warsaw visit was the arrival of Miss [Florence] Barrow, the former head of the relief Mission who had either shaped or brought into being most of its activities, so there was much consulting on many questions, and everyone who had known her was thrilled at her arrival. She determinedly acted fairy godmother and took us out to tea, to the picture gallery, and to a concert so that she got in more than business. The gallery consisted of one room of permanent pictures, and four of contemporary ones which are constantly changed; they are not wildly thrilling, - in fact you rather felt inclined to admire the perseverance of the authorities in continually trying all sorts of pictures in the hopes of some day finding something worth exposing. Two of the permanent pictures I liked awfully, one I've seen reproduced I think, - a marsh in a dim misty moonlight; the other was a woman lying asleep by a stream, - with the most perfect body and real out of door lights on it.

The concert was great; three violin concertos, Brahms, Prokofiev and Beethoven. Then there was an evening at bridge, [and] a lunch at the Young's when we were introduced to Margaret Sylvia, aged six weeks; she was a perfect pet, and I was allowed to put her to bed, but there wasn't time to see all of her that I should have liked. And on the last morning I went over Pany Jagmin's school, a secondary school for rather poorer girls. She had given me such a deprecating description of it that I expected something very sordid, but it was really very nice; obviously in an old and inconvenient building, but much what you would expect for a town secondary school that wasn't of the newest type. The girls looked jolly, were terrifically noisy when not actually working, but seemed to work with a will; I saw some of the art work, in which they were aiming at portraying movement rather than shape and had drawn all sorts of scenes, with little match stick figures, and a great deal of life they had managed to put into some of them; the singing was hearty and unmusical; and I was nearly green with envy at the accents and fluency of a fifth form doing French! Polish accent and intonation is almost exactly like French so I suppose it's very easy to get good results, but it sounds perfectly marvellous.

For an experiment I came back by the day train; it takes just about as long as the night journey but you have to change; and I must confess I've almost got acclimatized to the same extent as Jane who declares that a day journey is too boring, and an awful waste of time; she won't travel now except at night if she help it. The only thing is that if you are carrying money you have to keep such a careful eye on it at night, whereas in the daytime you can just read comfortably.

The day after I got back was spent partly in doing odds and ends, and partly in trying to leave my room in a state which might delude Miss Barrow into thinking I have a tidy nature, for she came on to visit us on the Thursday, and was to arrive while we were in Drohiczyn. Luckily just the week before the cotton needed to finish our new curtains which had been hung up since before Xmas, arrived and we had also planned to have some box covers made, so that although the house was not purposely decked out for the occasion, it was just at its best.

I think I must introduce you to the changes in our room. The living room has linen curtains with a red and black design in cross stitch, and the two boxes for weavings and the seat by the fire place covered with flaxen material striped with red and black, so the whole scheme is rather creamy colour with the unstained tables, and shelves, - it all looks very nice and clean. Then Miss Stankiewicz's room has brown and gold for its principal colours, Miss Golonowska's is all in green, mine in blue and orange, and Sophia Wrzeszcz's is supposed to have red and brown as its dominant colours, but really it looks the least furnished; she refuses to have it altered. The servants have had their rooms freshly white washed, and enlarged by the removal of the linen cupboard, and have them properly partitioned off by the old curtains from the living room, and following our example have made pictures from old magazines. Talking about pictures I have got a water colour drawing of some roses that a German girl who is studying art sent me, which I framed when I was in Warsaw, and they give the rippingest splash of colour to my walls.

You'll be glad to hear that Miss Barrow was duly impressed, - the first thing she said was that we had made a home out of the place, and the second was her admiration of its cleanliness (which you might think was a matter not generally remarked on by visitors, but which bucked us, particularly Miss Stankiewicz, up no end for the obstacles to such a state are manifold). I suppose honesty should compel me to add that Miss Barrow is the kind of person who would have found something pleasant to remark, whatever the state of the place, but of course we lapped it all up eagerly, - it's so nice to have an admiring audience, when you have just finished arranging something [end of letter missing].

xx xxx xx

Florence M. Barrow (1876–1964) Florence was born into a prominent Quaker family in Birmingham where her father was a businessman and mayor. She began a lifetime of work for the poor and disadvantaged by starting an adult literacy class for women at age 18, and then trained as a social worker at St Hilda's Settlement in Bethnal Green. Her first refugee work was with Serbians in France, after the Balkan War of 1912. She joined the first team of English Quakers sent to Russia in 1916 where her main job was managing an orphanage for refugee children. In 1919 she was part of a Quaker team sent to Germany to arrange delivery of family care packages from English relatives. She joined the Friend's Polish Unit in 1920 and in July 1921 was promoted to head the unit which she did until the main Mission wrapped up its work in March 1924. Back in Britain in 1924 she launched an organization to improve inner city housing. In 1932 she returned to refugee work in the Middle East, and in the later 1930s travelled to Nazi Germany as a Quaker 'secret agent' carrying messages to Jews. Returning to Britain in 1939 she spent most of the rest of her life working for better housing for the poor and marginalized. She died aged 82. [14, 29, 30]

22 March 1925, Horodec

Here Margaret describes a major local ceremony which brings together all the local power brokers, herself and the local staff, and even some local peasants to re-bury some soldiers killed in the war. Presumably an explanation about these dead soldiers was included in an earlier letter which is missing from this collection. The Vojt calls upon the prestige and resources of the Friends' project to allow him to entertain the visiting dignitaries in a style which he could not otherwise support. They are, after all, renting two of the biggest houses in the rebuilt town. We get some sense of Margaret's single-minded character as she does not for one moment consider postponing her 'distribution' work to accommodate this major request, but carries on with her work regardless. And much of the rest of the week seems to be taken up with difficulties created by a rigid adherence to her work plan, in the face of unexpected unfolding events. In the end help arrives, in the form of a Miss Czarnecka.

Dear People,

We have just lived through a hectic, and for Horodec, most wonderfully thrilling week. I don't think that any since I have been here has contained more crowded hours of glorious(?) life.

On Monday morning immediately after breakfast we received a visit from the Vojt and the Inspector, to inform us that there was going to be a great ceremony to bury the soldiers that had been brought to Horodec and which, as you may remember, have been lying in the barn for some time; the Starosta from Kobryn and the Archdeacon and lots of local celebrities and important officers were coming for the occasion, and, in short, please would we give them the use of our room for the lunch and cook it for them. That we were naturally perfectly willing to do, but they insisted that further we should act as hostesses which seemed extremely unnecessary especially as Tuesday is our distribution day and we couldn't spare the time.

However, as you can imagine, wonderful preparations were made for the feeding and accommodating about thirty people for meals, and for camping out some of the officers in the empty part of the house belonging to the Priest; by the afternoon Horodec was full of soldiers who marched round the village singing, accompanied by crowds of the school children and all the officers horses were tethered on our ground. On Tuesday morning we got up early and started our distribution at seven, in hopes of getting on with it, and as luck would have it, of course there was twice as much work coming in as usual. About eleven we stopped and went to the ceremony. First of all there was a mass in the Church; the Church was already full when we arrived and we stood at a side door, while crowds of people waited in the churchyard; after the Mass there was a procession to the grave side; the Priest chanted, and sprinkled all the coffins with holy water; then the band played, - a funeral march I suppose, though it sounded [like] music that wouldn't have been out of place in a tea room.

[second page of this letter typed on official letterhead] (I hope you admire our official note paper; the type writer has returned with another fiendish trick added to its little store and has caught and attempted to tear almost every line of the front page, so I am hoping this will be stronger. - As I have been carrying on official correspondence on my own paper for the last month, my conscience is quite happy about appropriating this.)

A colonel, then a civilian and finally a Priest spoke, all on the same theme, Sophia Wrzeszcz said, - that the soldiers had died for their country and that those present should be ready to follow their example. Salutes were fired over the graves and wreathes of green with red and white streamers, which the school children had brought were laid on each coffin. Whether I wasn't in the mood to be impressed I don't know, but I didn't feel that the whole ceremony was the least impressive; the ritual seemed artificial, and no real feeling of any kind behind it either as far as the religious and military side went, or from the point of view of the crowd. No one knew who the soldiers were so there was no personal regret, and it seemed as if the peasants, probably because they have seen too much of misery and of death to wonder at it were incapable of being stirred. They stood there, stolid looking and inert, didn't appear to listen to the speeches, - by that time they were all shuffling their feet, because it was a bitterly cold day. Their only sign of life came when the salute was fired, when the whole crowd of them threw their arms up protectingly over their heads and ducked as one man. It was just as though a wave had passed over them.

We returned to our distribution, but it was very soon time to make ourselves tidy and when Miss Stankiewicz came over to tell us that the Vojt had arranged the places and that I had to sit next to the Archdeacon, who was at the head of the first table, and Sophia Wrzeszcz next to the Starosta opposite to interpret any of my learned and interesting conversation, we wished more than ever that we had insisted on being excused. However we pulled ourselves together and determined to look as if we never did anything else or die. The room was full of people when we arrived. We were introduced all round and then took our places; luckily the Archdeacon knew enough French for us to get on with, and he wasn't difficult to talk to, though a little absent at moments; I think he was rather bored with having to be polite to me instead of talking to his cronies further down the table. The meal was interrupted with toasts, - the Archdeacon, the Starosta, the army and then me if you please. Every body stands up while they sing a 'For he's a jolly good fellow' kind of thing, and then you bow graciously to everyone who catches your eye as they hold up their glass to you. It all seemed so absurd and more like a dream than real life that I didn't even feel embarrassed, only rather amused.

The meal went on for ages, then we had a break when everyone was photographed by the grave, and then they all returned to the house for tea. Sophia Wrzeszcz departed to carry on the distribution, and I had still to cope with the Archdeacon. After another hour or so when talk had drifted to the work I suggested that he might like to go over and see what was being done, so he and an attendant priest trotted over to have a look at things, and I managed to lose them when they went to take their things off. But obviously no one had any idea of really leaving, although after the meal they had all bowed and kissed our hands and returned their thanks, and I struggled with some of the other guests in German and Polish. Bit by bit the awful realization dawned that they were expecting supper too! – a fact for which the Vojt had not prepared us. However, the kitchen rose to the occasion. Meanwhile I went to help finish the distribution which didn't finish till seven. Most of the guests went by train but some of the officers from the other table were left and the Vojt and wife and brother; they were a jolly, rather rowdy set, and after supper I suggested dancing. That might have been rather a brick, because I had forgotten it was Lent, at least I didn't realise that you must not dance in Lent, but everyone was so enthusiastic that I don't think it mattered.

After that some of them gave me an examination in Polish eked out with very bad German; I must say, I liked all the men who stayed behind, they jolly well put themselves out to be entertaining to everyone. One of the men I was most interested to meet is a man whose story all Poland has been ringing with. He is an Officer and was Governor of this county and last summer when the train he was in was attacked by bandits not very far from here, he ran away into the bushes, was found and robbed, even of part of his uniform I believe. Public opinion was very strong that although he may have been the only armed man on the train, he ought to have made some attempt at resisting what was after all an attack on the order of the province he was responsible for, and that as a soldier it was cowardly to submit to robbery. He was quite a young man, apparently a straight sort and he was making a most impassioned defence of his conduct after lunch to the people round, I did wish I could have understood what he said. I think he points out that it was only common sense to act as he did. He has been condemned to be degraded from the army, and has appealed. On the whole I think it is a fair sentence. He obviously didn't act in accordance with the military tradition of his country, and as an individual he is not being punished.

At the end, Mrs. Vojt gave us an invitation all to come over for Sunday and meet those of the rest of the party who live in the neighbourhood. We are probably going next week.

Miss Stankiewicz, who had managed the catering splendidly went to bed beaming with satisfaction at all the compliments showered upon her and delight at having moved in local society. She was priceless all day long, running around in a trembling dither, refusing to sit down for a second, refusing to eat a mouthful, and filled with apprehension lest anything should go wrong, - yet thrilled with the excitement and importance of her job. By Wednesday she was a wet rag.

Wednesday was equally hectic however. Sophia Wrzeszcz, who was leaving that day, had to combine a local distribution, special organization of the cutting, as all our stocks for Drohiczyn had got used up the day before, as well as trying to pack at intervals, while Miss Golonowska and I went in to the post for letters and money. I was expecting a most urgent letter from Jane, and we had sent in for it on Tuesday but it had not come and when we asked for letters, they gave me one, but not the one I expected with news, among other things, of money. There was no money waiting for us so I was forced to wire to ask her to bring some when she came the next day. The postman arrived after we did, and Miss Golonowska who watched him take the letters was convinced she saw some for us; so she went back some minutes later to ask him, and do you know he gave her ten in all with the date of Sunday, Monday, Tuesday and Wednesday stamped on different ones; and there was the one I expected from Jane which had been there since Monday, and which rendered the wire unnecessary. Do you know I had to pay for a form to write on to ask for that telegram back, and then they kept half of what had been paid for it? I was furious. The man was so insolent to Miss Golonowska too, - I am longing to write and complain, but Jane feels that would be very unwise.

The afternoon was a race against time to get enough out for the Drohiczyn distribution. I had decided to go in the next morning instead of the night before as there was so little cut and the last penny we had I wanted to send to Kobryn by Miss Golonowska to buy more linen. (A kit bag with linen had been sent to Kolpin instead of us so we were unexpectedly short.) Then suddenly at five o'clock Mr. Maluta from Kolpin turned up with the kit bag, and between trains wanted to see all the spare furmanka parts, etc. that might go to Kolpin and make arrangements about bringing the cinema here, one day. He had to be looked after, supper fitted in etc. last things finished up for Sophia Wrzeszcz, and behold, before he departed, Mr. Andronowski, the estate owner arrived, accompanied by a travelling friar whom he thought we might put up for the night in the room the officers had had.

That was all dismantled, - completely empty, so I bid a hasty farewell to the others who were all off to the station and got together things to furnish it once more, and had the fire lit. Unfortunately we couldn't rise to clean sheets, - we only possess eleven pairs for eight people, it is quite a matter of ingenuity to get regular changes and just this week in particular we had put up three visitors and were expecting another however it all looked very nice when we finished, and I led the monk who had a nice round red rosy face, to his rest, and retired to darn some necessary stockings for the morrow.

The next day when I came over to breakfast, Miss Stankiewicz met me in a great state of alarm. The Police had been, the monk had no proper papers, and was to be conducted to his destination and his identity gone into by the Police authorities. She was convinced we had entertained a Bolshevik spy, and said she had not been able to sleep all night from fear (although she knew nothing about his papers till the morning!) The last glimpse we had of our guest as we drove to the station was of him wandering along in the company of a Policeman.

I met Jane in the train and she helped me distribute; at seven we still hadn't finished and had to send some of the women home, telling them to come next Friday; yesterday and Friday, we have been discussing business. I have been trying to fit in Sophia Wrzeszcz's work as well as my own, and we have sold the horses, and discussed a scheme for renting and repairing the old estate house into the bargain. As I have said before it has been a record week.

Added to that Miss Czarnecka, the new lady arrived this morning. She is about thirty I should think, large and elegant with waved and shingled hair, a society manner and unlimited quantities of temperament. Jane and I both have queries in our minds as to how she will fit in. She has had the most violent experiences under the Bolsheviks, been ill twice with typhus, thrown out of a train in the snow and left to die. After various adventures, a fortnight after she was out of hospital she waded through an icy river up to her neck, escaping, - on Christmas eve, back into Poland, - a distance of ninety kilometres from where she was taken ill, done all through the snow on foot. She talks a lot and no doubt I shall be able to pass on 'the full story of my life' before very long.

Next week will be equally hectic I think, with her to initiate, and a great deal of last years work, etc. to clear up at Drohiczyn, and a two days distribution there. But the cheering thought of holidays is most sustaining, - I am getting off just before Easter, and having about a week in Breslau and ten days in and near Vienna. The weather today is glorious and if it is only anything like this we ought to have a heavenly time. My address to any one it may concern, form the 10th to the 17th will be bei Frl. Stenzel, Klosterstr. 14, Breslau 8; I don't yet know the Austrian one but letters will be forwarded from Warsaw, Widok 26, if they are marked 'please forward'.

Best wishes to all for the holidays, and love, Margaret.

3 May 1925, Horodec

Sadly, it turns out Miss Czarnecka is not cut out for work in the Industries, at least not as Margaret defines it. Margaret continues pushing forward at a hectic pace, and expecting everyone else to keep up with her, or be left by the wayside. But the rush is not only due to the pressure of work, but also because she is getting ready to leave on holiday.

The holiday provides a complete contrast with life and work in Horodec, and is marred only by the appearance of 'Bertie' the louse. Margaret is justifiably nervous about lice, not only from personal fastidiousness, but because lice carry typhus, a sometimes deadly disease which has killed several Quaker workers in the past few years and debilitated others.

Dear People,

I believe it is really only five or six weeks since I last wrote but it seems a whole lifetime. We had just had a truly hectic week when the Burial ceremony was conducted here, and from then until Easter I felt just like Alice in Wonderland when she was seized by the Duchess, ... faster and faster and faster. The distributions suddenly became nearly twice as large, there was all the work from the week before to make up, Sophia Wrzeszcz had gone, Miss Czarnecka had arrived. I put her in with the other factors, because if she did not actually make extra work the amount of nervous energy she exhausted in us all is unbelievable. If I tried from now till next year to describe her adequately I am afraid you would still be far from any real idea of what she was like, and you wouldn't get her against the background that the rest of us did, - getting up at six, working late and at top speed to get through. "I am never so happy as when I am working" she assured us at frequent intervals during the day, - and one could almost believe it as one watched her, spending a day and a half typing seven copies of a letter (with carbons) or sorting collars with languorous movements, like a slow motion cinema picture, - enlivening her labours and interrupting ours, with ceaseless and vaguely irrelevant prattle. She nearly drove us distracted at distributions when she interrupted every calculation about cottons, wages, etc. with requests for information to which she never never listened beyond the first half sentence, darting off in the middle to ask whether we did not think a combination of orange and purple perfectly fascinating? She invariably got up late for breakfast, arriving in a somewhat frayed semi evening dress, and fulminating against the manners of the villages who were so remiss as to stare in at her window when she did what she called her gymnastics in an unclad state; she appeared in curl papers on the Sunday we were invited to the Vojt's in the afternoon, - and I could relate still choicer details about her, but they are not entirely suitable for publication.

Apart from her mannerisms however, - she no more entered into the spirit of carrying on an Industry than she was capable of flying, and she was not either loyal or really straight, so we very soon realized she would have to go. It was an awful shock to her, - one that she could not absorb either then or since, that she could be unsuitable and she spent the whole evening arguing the matter. I felt very sorry for her, she so obviously thought I was merely prejudiced, and if only she stayed longer I should soon see how valuable she really was, and she had quarrelled with her friends in Warsaw which made it rather awkward for her. She asked if she might appeal to Jane, - or threaten her, whichever way you like to look at it, pointing out that she was entitled to three months notice. I consented, but Jane imagining I was going to push the lady off did not reply for some days and when she did we had a scene which would beat any novel for being truly theatrical.

When I saw Miss Czarnecka was contemplating refusing to move, I said firmly "The horses will be ready for you at eight tonight", and swept from the room. We had a further instalment at supper when she represented Jane and myself as being in league to defraud her of her rights, and when I tore up a certificate of service that she had written out for herself on official note paper she had abstracted from my desk without permission.

Since she has been back in Warsaw her claims have been settle in regards money, but she is publishing abroad legends of our kicking peasants etc.!!! Oh but she was a wonderful woman.

I pushed her off on the Wednesday, and started myself on Good Friday. It was an appalling journey, one extra each side and about four standing in the middle. Everyone in vile tempers swearing at each station at the poor distracted souls who were desperately trying to find their way in somewhere. At Brzesc the Conductor tried, and failed to turn out four men who were in the (ladies) carriage, and enlisted the help of three armed Police before they would move. After much undignified exchange of repartee on both sides the men departed only to return by the two doors and the corridor as soon as the train moved off. It was about this point that I realized the presence of Bertie who had attached himself fondly to me. It was useless to hunt him down then; as soon as I got to Warsaw I took my quarterly bath, and indulged in a thorough but fruitless search so I concluded he must have continued his travels.

I squeezed in two hours sleep, breakfast, a confab with Jane, a visit to the Office, and hair cut and set out in an equally crowded train to Breslau, - but here the charming manners, at any rate of one couple, made me repent of my generalizations on Polish manners the night before. Anyway as time went on there were fewer and fewer people travelling, and by night time I was quite alone in the carriage. Else [Stenzel] met me at the station, and by half past one we were happily in bed. It WAS jolly being in a large and 'lustig' family again. We had to hunt for Easter eggs, and every one had a little group of chocolate ones, with hares, or chickens, set out on a special table, and a tiny glass of violets which were used as a table decoration at lunch and which guarded the eggs the rest of the time.

It was a very happy week; no one could have been more friendly or more hospitable, and the multitude of things we did would take too long to tell. We explored the town (doing special research on hat shops), and the country round (doing dittos on tea gardens) and made all sorts of music with piano, violins and voices. On Easter Monday we went to see the Heilege Johanna (translated by Else as 'the Holy Jane') [Joan of Arc?]

which was extremely well played, I thought. Joan was very attractive, boyishly natural, and with a convincing streak of dreamy visionary, but nothing much of the rough country girl about her. I was awfully interested to see it as I have only read it in English. It also made it easier for me to follow because it was the first play I have seen in German.

Breslau is a very pleasant city; it isn't strikingly picturesque in any way, but it is clean, spacious and dignified; plenty of parks and green spaces, with charming walks by the river, and the waters of what used to be the moat. Apart from the old Ratheus [Town Hall] most of it seems to be fairly modern. The University is fairly old I suppose, - it is a fine building but it doesn't wear an air of great age.

Of course time was much too short; it was sad to tear oneself away, but we were no more successful than Elvire in beseeching it to stay its course... Oh but I have forgotten to tell you the sequel about Bertie. Excuse this seeming irrelevance, but such a thing has never happened to me before and I trust will never again. Two days after I arrived I was forced to the reluctant and horrified conclusion that Bertie was still with me. But where? ... Not in my clothes, - I wasn't wearing the same ones, not in my bed, as far as I could see, more vain searches; - the next day further evidence!... still no success; and the next day, when I had given up attempts, I saw him doing a perfect marathon round the corner of the blanket! I summoned the family to witness his execution, and assured Frau Stenzel who was deeply shocked, that I knew I had brought him with me. My one hope, and hers is that he has left no survivor, but I feel after this little incident, that if I was ever before likely to be branded as respectable, I shall now have escaped that for ever!

The journey to Vienna was also fraught with incident. They had sold out of tickets in Vienna, and had three different ideas as to what train was running, so that I had to do a stage at the time, and hope for the best; I crossed two frontiers, took six tickets, with three different kinds of money, and changed four times. The piece through Czechoslovakia was fascinating, we went higher and higher, and I nearly stood up and yelled at the sight of the Carpathians, - my first really truly mountains. Breslau had been a change for Horodec in the sense of town versus country and home life versus the Industry, but here was a different kind of country, hills and rivers, instead of flat marshes, and live flowers and trees and Spring, instead of dead grass and bare boughs. It was the most heavenly day, too, in which to see it all.

The hotel in Vienna was quite a long way from the station so I saw something of the city on the way. After getting thoroughly cleaned and rested, I set out to the West station where Billy was due to arrive at 9:50. It was quite a long tram ride, but I got there at half past nine, - strayed onto the departure side first, and was rather taken aback at being told to hurry because the train had already come in. I wandered out into the street again and got to the other side to find the whole station deserted, and the doors on to the platform locked, no sign of any passengers or even an official. A porter in the luggage office said that the train had come in at 9:20, and every one had been gone ten minutes.

Feeling very wild and penitent at having missed Billy I seized a taxi in which to chase after her to the hotel, - but there, no-one had arrived. Picture my emotion! "Alone in Vienna, - or lost in a railway station"! I besought the manager to tell me if there was another station at which the train might have arrived, - so he phoned up and discovered that there was still a possible train at the West at 10:55; a gleam of hope lit up my haggard eye, and I boarded the tram feeling that the worst might not have happened. They unlocked the station doors to let off a few passengers, and pushed me firmly but gently through to lock them again as I still stood watching if anyone was coming off. Luckily the sequel to this wild tale is no 'oribble murder; the explanation is not even exciting; the train had duly arrived at 9:50 but at the East station for some unknown reason, and this time Billy was safe in bed when I got back.

We went off the next afternoon to Gloggnitz, and spent the most heavenly week there. We stayed at a nice old fashioned hotel height [sic] the Sohwarzen Alder, and led a perfectly and utterly restful existence, - so did the personnel of the place, judging by the time they took serving meals. Anyway we got up late, set out, with food, for the whole day, and walked and lazed alternately, as the spirit moved us. The Austrian Tourist Club has blazed trails on all the little paths over the hills, so that you can wander almost anywhere, and know where you are going. The country is a network of tall steep hills, and winding valleys, some deep, and others gentle and broad, and it was fascinating climbing up the little zig-zag paths, and seeing the face of the country change from each different outlook. We didn't attempt to reach the two mountains, the Schneeberg, and Raxalpe, whose dark, snowy heights overtopped the other hills; I suspect it would have been very difficult, for in spite of what anyone can say, I am convinced they changed their positions every hour or so, - they were always appearing in some totally different direction from the one in which they had last been seen.

Everything was a joy; - the slanting sunlight through dim and fragrant pine woods; the fresh young green and clear gray of the beech trees; orchards yellow with tall cowslips; and grassy spaces with patches of violets and forget-me-nots, - and even once a field of gentians; being on top of things, drinking in the air and the sun, watching the mist or shadow slip down from the hill and chase over the valley, through the swaying branches of a larch or a pine; and feeling the hills grow still and the peace deepen with night fall.

Our most thrilling walk was the last afternoon through the pouring rain, - a long gorge winding through tall, grey, forest crowned cliffs, with a small green torrent rushing along over the stones at the foot, and a glimpse at turns in the road of an old ruined castle on the top of a rock, once the lair of robber barons as they lay in wait for merchants passing through the hills to Vienna.

I had to get back to Warsaw two days earlier than I had planned because of a KPPKW Committee so Vienna has to be crowded out except for the days passing through it. We managed to see the outside of most of the buildings in the centre of the city. They are finely spaced and some of them are beautiful. It would be nice to know Vienna more thoroughly. But as I said before, it was a heavenly week.

Spring arrived here while I was away, though things are not as far out as they were in Austria, and I am beginning to feel I may even get attached to Horodec. But such a noise you never heard; all the trees round are filled with crows who give voice incessantly; all the marshy spots with frogs, who vie with the crows, and above it all there are cuckoos, (one with three notes) and the storks, who join in form time to time; the combined effect is terrific. The storks arrived before I went away, - heaps and heaps of them. They seem credible when you watch them on their nests, but when they fly down and walk about in the road or round the house they give me the same feeling that I am sure people must have when they start seeing snakes and things, - they seem so incongruous to the rest of the picture that I can't believe they are really there.

Sophia Wrzeszcz's sister has come to take her place, and we are making all sorts of plans for walks and picnics, and swimming in the canal; she seems very game for everything. There is really lots more to tell, but I must stop now; time has been rather taken up to day by entertaining the Vojt and the school mistress from Mechodowicze to lunch, most of the afternoon and to supper, - and we are shortly going to visit a ball that is being held in the school to celebrate their Constitution day; - the schools have been having great doings all the afternoon.

Much love to everyone, Margaret.

27 May 1925, Horodec

With the arrival of spring, Margaret begins to take more note of the landscape and the people. She goes out to the surrounding villages, chasing after more of that missing cotton, but is disappointed when the local Soltys doesn't back up her version of justice.

She mentions a trip to Warsaw that the project has arranged for the girls who weave on the project looms. The trip was a success and was repeated annually for several years, leading eventually to an exchange between some Polish students from Warsaw and the Belarusian girls in Horodec, and fulfilling one of the Friends' goals of promoting understanding between peoples and breaking down class barriers. [17]

Margaret closes the letter with a story she hears from a peasant woman on the train. This story bears all the hallmarks of an 'urban legend' but Margaret passes it on as if it is true. The tale is almost certainly apocryphal, but the telling of it says a lot about the fears of the older peasants about their children becoming estranged and corrupted by the abruptly changing world. The role of the Jew, presented as the ultimate beneficiary of the peasant family's misfortune, is also very revealing of peasant prejudices.

Dear People,

I wonder what was the date of my last letter? It can't have been more than three weeks ago, but since then we have lived through all the spring, and half the summer. I have never seen things change with such rapidity, - and you wouldn't recognize Horodec as the same place as in the winter. Right until Easter the village and all the country round looked waste, unkempt, and desolate. There were no gardens, no fields, not the smallest sign of cultivation; then suddenly about Easter time, people began to be active. They ploughed the little bits of ground round their houses, dug and planted it, put up fences, swept the bit of lane near them and generally had a spring clean out as well as in. Most of the plain round the town was ploughed, parts that had been more or less under water the whole of the winter, and suddenly everywhere the desert began to blossom. First cowslips, violets, lilac and fruit blossom; hardly before we had time to realize that they were there, they were gone and the swamp places were thick with yellow irises, the drier parts white with cow parsley, and the rye knee deep. Now the irises are over, there are yellow water lilies, purple orchises, white cotton grass, and corn flowers, while the rye we passed between this morning was higher in places than the horses. With the warm weather the children came out. Those and little pigs! The place swarms with them. The former are dressed in the weirdest variety of costume, but most of the small girls wear white handkerchiefs like their mothers and every where you meet a diminutive form brandishing a stick after a small group of ducks or geese or pigs. I'm hoping later to get some more photos.

The rooks continue their awful din which makes it impossible to get any peace near the house, except at night, when the nightingales are glorious. So far we have evaded flies here but I expect they will begin soon, and the mosquitoes have hardly made themselves felt, except for one short week. The sun is scorching. Our great joy is bathing in the canal, - had we started when I last wrote? The water is as warm as can be so that you can stay in as long as you like; it isn't very deep, but quite deep enough to swim, and it's a yellow brown colour! The greatest trial are the weeds if you try to leave the one spot. There has been no rain worth mentioning for weeks and weeks and the canal is lower than usual, and the long weeds tie themselves around ones legs.

Some days there is hardly any room for long chains of rafts to go down; the canal links up the Baltic and the Black Sea. I don't know if the wood goes all the way; but the timber men have little straw thatched cabins built on top of the raft, - the rest of which generally seems to be swimming in water; it must take them weeks, for they move very slowly. Today we interrupted a bathing party of about twenty who were going in grandmothers, daughters and grandchildren apparently, two or three at a time. They seem to combine their weeks washing with their personal ablutions; they make no attempt to swim, but stand knee deep in water and have a good old bath. I imagine it takes some time to dig down through their winter layers. The common method of ablutions, - I forget if I have told you this, is to take a mouthful of cold water, - keeping it until it is almost warm, eject it carefully on whatever part of ones anatomy requires attention, and finish with a polish from a towel; babies are always washed this way, if their mothers risk washing them at all in the winter. It is also the common method of sprinkling the linen ready for ironing.

I had rather imagined from these accounts that the peasants were averse to water, but it is evidently not so. One evening when a visitor from Warsaw was here we walked down to the canal at about seven and she was so taken aback that we beat a hasty retreat; all down the river, both sides of the bridge, was far as the eye could see were human forms in various stages of undress. The crowd today was very mystified by our [swimming] costumes and thought that as we went without being decently undressed or decently clad in skirts, we must be men; they watched every detail of our dressing with the greatest interest, - couldn't for the life of them make out what my suspender belt was, and opined that I must be a lot richer than Sophia Wrzeszcz because I wore two frocks (i.e. a dress and a petticoat).

At last a Priest has come; not one of those we had met before, but a young, gay, and energetic individual. He has already had the Church thoroughly cleaned and white washed, the windows cleaned, the holes in the ground outside filled in, and he talks of having a croquet lawn made, and Miss Wrzeszcz is persuading [him] to have a court made for tennis at the same time (not that there is enough space for one really, but she is aching to hit a ball across a piece of string, and he is going to have the ground flattened out for her). She by the way is a young lady of much temperament and resource. She isn't as capable or conscientious as her sister I think, - but is generally in great spirits and makes the most of very available source of amusement. She calls on everyone she has ever been introduced to; borrows or hires a horse and rides, goes on the river in a leaky ferry boat, is always game for a swim, and is planning to play tennis and croquet.

When however her high spirits forsake her she goes into the blackest depths of despondency, - suddenly takes to smoking, consumes twenty cigarettes or more a day, and she confided to me that she takes to drinking as well 'when she is in a bad humour' as she puts it. There have been no visible signs of her having done so here so far,

[text/page missing - apparently describing Miss Golonowska going home for her father's funeral] ...some weeks ago, and so she went home for a week, and seems to have had a thoroughly harrowing time. She came back to Poland years after the others and was the only one who really kept up with her father, who had separated from her mother twelve years ago because they couldn't get on. But the mother apparently had done nothing but weep and pr? some fresh letter from or about the father daily; he has left a wife younger than Miss Golonowska, and a three year old child, and has written to her to ask her to help them.

Miss Wrzeszcz as you can imagine is very bracing for her, most of the time, at any rate. The two of them have started teaching Polish to five of our workers (the people hereabouts speak White Russian) and not all of them know how to read and write that). I have been caught by this wave of enthusiasm for adult education sufficiently to undertake to teach Miss Stankiewicz English. I think it will be pricelessly funny. She is going to buy a Berlitz method while she is in Warsaw. She is there at the moment with twelve of the loom girls for three days; they are seeing Warsaw, going to the theatre, and a cinema, and visiting some of the big shops. I would give a good deal to understand their accounts and comments, - they have talked of nothing else for weeks past. Jane is offering a prize for the best account, but I don't think there will be many entries, - only one or two of them can write.

We had a very exciting distribution yesterday; in fact few since I came back after Easter have been really pleasant; something wild seems to have happened to Miss Golonowska's calculations, and she gave out too much cotton in most cases, though in some cases far too little, - and of course

The loom girls visit Warsaw, May 1925. *The project employed a group of young women to weave blankets, bedspreads, placemats, etc. In an attempt to broaden their experience and outlook, they were taken on a holiday in Warsaw, where they visited museums, the botanical gardens, and the riverside water front.*

the peasants have seized the opportunity to steal. They are always frightfully indignant when you accuse them and refuse to pay them until they return the rest, and five women yesterday kicked up an awful row. Miss Wrzeszcz isn't at all good at shutting them up either. They demanded their work back and came round behind the table to where the work was lying. I interposed my stalwart form and felt exactly like Horiatis as I defied them to touch it; they had three goes at us, but didn't dare rush me, and then a little later when Miss Wrzeszcz was by it they seized their things without her making the slightest effort to prevent them. I was annoyed, because she only needed to have stood in front. However, short of using physical force we couldn't tear the things from them and we warned them we would come after them today.

So this morning we set out for Kamien Krolewski, and got the Soltys, the head Pan of the village, to call them for us; they came and half the village with them to listen to it all. I wish you could have heard it, it was priceless; they all talked at once, - told different stories about the cotton every time and the Soltys was absolutely no good at all; he didn't attempt to say much, but when he did they just howled him down, and refused to give up the work. We had to leave without it apparently in ignominious defeat, - but the day of reckoning will come later, - because I have refused to pay them for their work unless they gave it then and there; they are in possession of a runner or two, which will not be exceedingly useful to them, - and the money they would have had for their bonus will more than pay for the material in the things.

After that we drove across the fields to the other Kamien, Kamien Szlacheczki, a much more pleasant experience. It is a fascinating village down a long street; each tiny thatched cottage is under the shelter of a huge, protective looking tree; there was linen out every where on the fences hung on the side of the house or flat on the patches of grass; some of it this years, some in the form of shirts; the black pots of different and beautiful shapes, in which they keep their sour milk, were also hanging upside down on the spikes of most of the houses , and every here and there storks were sitting on the ends of the roofs in their low flat nests. Little groups of women were sitting on the roadside, embroidering, or standing gossiping in their yards, and hailed us with great friendliness (some of these were equally capable of stealing cotton and of being just as abusive as the others, but they don't happened to be the ones at the moment, an these little scenes are generally sans rancune).

It looked such a peaceful, rural scene, - but there is an awfully grim side to these people; one Sunday, a little while ago, we went to the estate owner [Antoni Wyslouch] at Pirkowicze, where the Mission used to be, and he had been awfully good to his peasants before the war; the Germans came, and occupied his house for a year or two, treating the place carefully, then the Cossacks came, and they left it unharmed, - but while the fighting was going on the peasants came and carried away everything they could move, - including doors and wood work, - and the same thing happened in many cases. One day before Easter I went in the same train with a peasant from Kamien Szlacheczki who was going to complain about her son who had refused to obey her; and when we seemed a little surprised at that, she said she was a widow, and had to protect herself. And she told us what had happened a week before in the same village.

There had been an old man living there with his two sons; he was getting very old and weak, and they were impatient to inherit the piece of land he owned. So they said to him, "If you die, we shall have to pay a lot of money to inherit your land, - it would be much better to give it to us now, - you are too old to work it, - and we will keep you." The old man saw the force of the argument, - he was no believer in taxes, and he went with the two sons to the Gmina to make out the deed of gift; then he went home, while the two men went to look at their new property. On the way there, one said to the other; "You had better look after our father, - you are married and have a wife to cook for you." "No, - you are the one, I have children, and greater expenses," and a quarrel began. They cursed the fact of having to provide for the old man, and the thought struck one, why not kill him and be rid of him. And on the way back from the field itself, they planned to hang him. It was the work of a few minutes to find the rope, and they had barely finished their deed when they heard someone coming, and ran to hide. A young Jew was passing and happened to glance towards the stable door; the old man was beyond speech but his agonized eyes shewed that he was not quite dead, and the Jew hastened to cut him down. He could not speak but when he was sufficiently recovered to walk with a little help, they went together to the Gmina where he managed to make them understand by signs what had happened. The Soltys asked him to go into a room at the back to rest, and sent a message to the two sons to bring their father to the Gmina as there was a hitch in the deed of gift and his signature was required. Now they were in a quandary; neither dared go back to survey their finished work, and they decided to bribe another old man of the village to say he was their father. The Soltys looked at them for a moment, then quietly opened the door at the back and their father appeared; they gave themselves away completely, at seeing what they thought was their father's ghost, and they were shot the next morning; justice in these parts seems to be swift. We said we were surprised they should both be sentenced to death for what proved to be only an attempted murder (though really as far as they were concerned there was no difference) but the peasant woman seemed to think that it was quite the right thing to have happened, and in her case she wasn't going to let it get to that stage; she was going to have her son obey her right away.

Tomorrow I am going down to Warsaw until Sunday night. On Sunday I am going with Edith Hall, an old Mission worker who is out here to see the Whit Sunday Procession of peasants at a place near Warsaw where they still wear the old traditional costumes, much more brightly coloured than in this part of the world.

Oh I always forget the climax to my stories; it rather rounds off the whole episode of the old man and his sons to know that the Jew inherited the land!

Much love to everyone, Margaret

17 June 1925, Horodec

Margaret sets up a stall to display the work produced by the project at an exhibition in the nearest town, Kobryn, 13 miles west along the railroad. She just misses meeting the most famous man in Poland.

After more than six months on the job, Margaret has formed some firm ideas about the development of the project and the Industry. When three senior representatives of the Friends' Council for International Service (CIS) arrive for a field visit, she shares her opinions freely and frankly. We don't know if she has any ambitions to continue her work with the Friends at this point, but entering into 'furious arguments' with the key spokesman can't have advanced that cause. But Margaret's disillusionment has got the better of her.

The letter concludes in Warsaw where the KPPKW Committee has to make difficult decisions about laying off local staff and renewing the lease on the Priest's house.

Dear People,

Comparative calm once more, and I take up my pen, I mean my typewriter to greet you!

The week before the exhibition was a very full one, because Miss Golonowska was down with malaria, and all our spare time was spent in entertaining or being entertained by the members of the military service commission who were here for a week.

Their presence distracted the thoughts of the staff very considerably, and I began to wonder if we should ever get safely there; on the last morning I only just discovered that Miss Stankiewicz was sending off two looms in about forty different parts without a single label to one of them, - in spite of the fact that I had given her the special address we were requested to use. Sending the looms was in response to a visit [to Horodec] while I was in Warsaw from one of the officials of the exhibition who had undertaken to pay all transport expenses and to arrange accommodation for the workers.

The exhibition was to begin at 9 a.m. on Sunday morning so we took the morning train on Saturday, and arrived at the office about 11. After some searching we found the man who had called about the looms, and he took us to the office while we waited for horses to take our luggage to the station. It was a small and crowded place; people hurried in and out making hectic enquiries, - the secretary himself seemed in a feverish state of losing his temper continually, and only just managing to recover it; none of the cards were ready, and we had to wait while the typist received instructions as to how to register us. After about an hour the loom man said that horses were there, so we followed him to the station; another weary wait of forty five minutes and we succeeded in getting our goods; by the time we got back to the office the committee member in charge of accommodation had arrived, - and he proceeded to allot us our rooms. Hungry, and a little weary, we sought some lunch, and then inspected our room. Bare boards, a wooden box with an enamel basin of doubtful cleanliness for a washstand, two chairs, and a table covered with American cloth, with a wardrobe in a corner to give an air of respectability to the place. It might have been much worse, - but the price they had the cheek to charge!!! They charged for the room, for each set of sheets, for each towel, for electric light, which was not available, so much for taking away your passport for registering, three times as much for returning it, so much for service, so much for a town tax for something else, - I've forgotten what, ... and with the total you probably could stay in a first class hotel anywhere else. Luckily we had a slight reduction on account of being exhibitors.

Hotel inspection finished, we returned to the exhibition, seized our luggage, begged to know where we were to put up our stall, but the committee member who arranged places had not arrived, so there we sat the whole afternoon waiting for the gentleman and cussing loudly at intervals. Many people had already found out their sites, I do not know how, and were busy erecting stalls of putting out their machinery. The

Kobryn Exhibition, June 1925. *Margaret spends a Sunday supervising a stall at a government sponsored exhibition selling woven and embroidered products produced by her project. The stall was constructed by a local carpenter and set up in an open yard decorated with young birch trees. The ex-president of Poland, Józef Pilsudski caused some excitement when he visited the stall.*

ground was just a waste yard, with big white washed barns round it, and a great many young birch tress had been cut down and stuck round to try and make it look more elegant; finally at half past four we were shown our corner, and began to have a stall put up. No tables were provided. We had to employ our own carpenter, - and though this of course delayed things because he had to saw every bit of wood he was going to use, and was more expensive, the three tiered arrangement he erected was far more effective shewing off our things. We had our choice of two halves of a space, and bagged one with a wall behind just a foot or two higher than the table, and it made a find background of rug. Above that still we hung a line for one or two of the choicest things we wanted to display, and in the corner at the back we hung some of the woven curtains. The whole effect was most satisfactory.

There was an elaborate programme prepared, but of course as stall holders we had little chance of following it; we decided however to attend the church service which began the proceedings, and arrived at 9.15 to find mass going on, and a crowded church. We stood at the back, for a little while, and then I sat outside and waited for Miss Wrzeszcz; as you may remember I mentioned that the beginning was to be at nine, so you will appreciate the point when I tell you that, near the exhibition itself, we met the procession with band setting out, - at about a quarter to ten for the service.

There were a fair number of people that morning, they came and looked and questioned, but hardly anyone bought. The aristocracy here despise embroideries as being peasanty, - and though they are willing to admire them as work, do not prize them as possessions, and it was rather comical to see them nearly all drift towards the table next to us, to admire a sickly table centre, on canvas with pink roses and bilious green leaves. During the morning we had two invitations to lunch, - the first from the Doctor who had attended to Miss Golonowska, and whom we had seen a good deal of during the week, and the second from three of the local youths; they were fearfully annoyed that they had been forestalled, hung about until they met us going off with the Doctor, and joined us without being invited, which I thought extremely cool; I think they did actually feel ashamed of themselves when the Doctor insisted on paying, to the extent of a whole weeks pay, as they very well realized. For he did us proud. I had special Polish things – a kind of jellied fish, with tiny tiny lobsters, which I couldn't manage at all, then a cold soup, made of pink cream, and thick with bits of cucumber, spring onion, shell fish of some kind, and I don't know what else; it was very sumptuous but too rich to consume it all so I skipped the meat course, and ended up with a strawberry Melba.

Next morning we arrived at the exhibition to find Jane Pontefract, with William Albright, T. Edmond Harvey and Henry Harris, - great personages of the C.I.S. They were on their way to Kolpin, and were to pay us a visit later in the week. There were fewer people on the ground the second day, and all together we only sold about three pounds worth of things; in the afternoon the great Pilsudski visited the exhibition; he, unlike all the other people was there half an hour before he was reported to be coming so Jane and I were having tea, instead of by the stall, where he admired a red cloth for nearly five minutes, according to Miss Wrzeszcz. (In case you don't know who Pilsudski is, I may inform you that he is a celebrated Polish President, - I did not know, before I came to Poland.) We saw him afterwards quite plainly; he looked inexpressibly weary, - his eyes were utterly lifeless, but he has a dignified and soldierly bearing.

The only sequels to the exhibition are that they charged us for half as much space again as we reserved and the official who invited us to bring the looms, had no authority to offer freight and disappeared without either arrangement or apology; we heard it rumoured on the Monday that our stall had been awarded a prize, - apparently several people have heard so, but it hasn't materialized to date.

Jane came back with us [to Horodec] the next day; and on Friday the great trio arrived, or rather on Thursday night. They came partly to look into the housing situation; Jane had urged it on them so that they should be convinced of the necessity of advancing money in London to build a house. In reality that question has been settled already in

London, but the letter that had been written had been misleading. So what really happened was that they spent the whole day trotting round, inspecting premises, and after great deliberation feeling prepared to recommend to the Committee that we should take a little house on the green for our loom room instead of the two we now have, - a conclusion which would be obvious to almost anyone! I am afraid I spent the day being either thoroughly aggressive or flippant. In some ways they so utterly fail to grasp the realities of this work and these people.

And Edmund Harvey, their spokesman is that terrible kind of person who gushes in a soapy manner over everything, and simply oozes brother love, without considering in the least the personality of the persons round him; we had a few furious arguments, - one when he suggested housing in a house on the green and suggesting that two workers could perfectly well share a room at the back, - a room which would give them a space of about eight square feet with a big corner eaten out by the stove; he seemed to think that because he roughed it once while doing emergency work in France that workers here should be glad to put up with any corner that is found for them. He seems to have not the slightest feeling that this is a new thing being built up, where it is possible for us to set at least a decent standard of living for the workers. It's true there is no money for it in the Industry and that we have possibly over produced this year, but [text missing] there all right and if the Industry were not going to support the workers in decent conditions, and moreover soon be capable of paying bigger wages to the peasants, it would in my opinion be better to chuck it altogether. I do think the work itself is worth producing, but not at the price of present conditions. Of course I hope that bit by bit as it really gets started wages will be raised.

We argued this point too; - but E. H. thinks that we are conferring a benefit on the dear peasants simply by giving them something to do, - so nice for them to enjoy a little gossip the day they come to the distribution, - a sort of holiday for them, - yes waiting for hours huddled together in the snow or cold or the rain, - or lying about on the ground dozing when the weather is finer!! wasting a whole day to get about four and six [shillings] for a week's work.

He also criticised the fact that I hadn't called on the Russian Priest to ascertain his precise religious views, and reproved me (unjustly) for telling a lie to the Jew, so altogether we can't be said to have spent a very friendly day. The others were much quieter and left all the talking to him, so I didn't really discover until the weekend, that they are not necessarily of one mind; in fact I think they smile a little smile inside them. William Albright is a sport, - he is practically crippled with rheumatism but doesn't let that make any difference. He clambers round everywhere, and takes a detailed interest in everything although you can see him go absolutely stiff, after he has been in the same position for a little while.

Henry Harris, who is taking Wilmer Young's place in Warsaw is rather a dear, - a sort of E.V. Lucas or J.M. Barrie bachelor uncle (though he is married by the way) with a great sense of humour and a rather more cheerful view of things, - at any rate of the Industries position than either of the others. I am going to housekeep for him at the end of July, and shall discover if there is very much more to him than those two qualities. I find it so far difficult to conjecture.

[Back in Warsaw] I went to a jolly At Home on Saturday night, where a Miss Maleska, - I forget if I told you about her before, - played three things of Chopin's simply rippingly; all Monday was spent committing; a most depressing meeting in the morning at which it was suggested that we had exhausted the embroidery market in England and had better close down centres and not open again till December. I won't bore you with all the arguments for and against. At any rate Miss Wrzeszcz and Miss Golonowska have been given notice; Vera the loom girl with us is to go, the cook is to be sent home for the summer and Miss Stankiewicz and I are to keep things going in part of Vinograd's house where we only sleep at present; we can't re-rent the Priest's house. Kolpin to is likely to suffer, and unless funds can be found for it in Poland, will have to be handed over to the Ministry of Agriculture.

Did you know there were real pied pipers in Poland; there are probably three, and they are really employed to charm the rats away from a village. There are only three more weeks of distribution now; then will come the pleasant job of taking the bonus to the villages.

Love to all, Margaret

xx xxx xx

Józef Pilsudski (1867–1935) Born into the nobility, but raised in genteel poverty, Pilsudski grew up in Vilna, Lithuania under the Russian Empire. A student socialist, he spent five years in exile in Siberia. In World War One he created the Polish Legion which fought under the Austro-Hungarians on the side of Germany. From 1918–22 he was the first Chief of State of the reconstituted Poland. He led the Polish army through the Polish-Soviet War 1919–21, and dominated politics through to 1923. Hailed by many as the founder of modern Poland, he was probably the most famous man in Poland in 1925. Technically retired, he still exerted considerable influence in the political backrooms and in 1926 he led a coup and took control of the country again. He remained in various positions of power until he died in 1935. [18, 31]

Thomas Edmund Harvey (1875–1955) Edmund was an English Quaker from Leeds. He graduated from Oxford and studied at the University of Berlin and at the Sorbonne. He began his career with the British Museum, but was most interested in social reform issues, including prison reform, poverty alleviation and welfare. He entered politics at the municipal level in London in 1904, and rose to national politics as a Liberal MP for Leeds in 1910. As a Quaker he was a pacifist and helped write the legislation which legalized the position of conscientious objectors in the British Army during World War One. In 1914 he suggested setting up the Friends' War Victims Relief Committee, and then became one of its first volunteers in France during World War One. He was in and out of Parliament, and in 1925 was not a sitting member. He was asked by the Council for International Service to visit Poland on their behalf in 1925. From 1937 to 1945 he was MP for the Combined Universities seat, and took a particular interest in the plight of academic refugees. [14]

William Albright (1853–1942) Born in a Quaker family in Birmingham, William apprenticed to an iron-masters before entering his father's business of chemical manufacturing. During his life he managed the large family firm and was a magistrate. He championed causes as varied as: allotments for the unemployed, visiting conscientious objectors, adult education in England, and the question of slave labour in West Africa. A man of principle, in 1915 he resigned the chairmanship of the family firm because he would not share in profits generated by the war. From 1914 he was the first chairman of the Friends' War Victims Relief Committee and he continued to support the subsequent Council of International Service and Friends' Service Council. He served on the Council of the Quaker's Woodbrooke College in Birmingham for more than 30 years. He married in his 40s and had no children and died in 1942 at the age of 89. [22]

11 July 1925, Horodec

Now into her last month in the field, Margaret's patience is wearing thin. She has no sympathy for the 'work to rule' approach adopted by her two local staff who are being laid off, and seems to expect them to show commitment to the job despite the fact that the organisation is not showing commitment to them.

Margaret's final days are taken up with delivering annual bonus payments to the women embroiderers. The calculations are complicated and include a confusing element of 'collective punishment' for work not returned by the village, deducted from a bonus earned on individual work. Margaret recognises that the project recordkeeping is inadequate and she seems frustrated by her desire to make something objective out of what is inevitably a very subjective calculation. She tries to use the local village leader – the Soltys – to put pressure on the women who have not returned work, and she is disappointed to find that Belarusian peasant women don't 'respect authority' – the Solty's or hers. But visiting the villages is clearly an adventure worth the trouble. And she is leaving the area all too soon anyway.

Dear People,

I had been hoping to be able to greet you joyfully, - by Monday at any rate with 'Now the labourers' task is o'er' ... But alas it is not so... anything but!!!

About three or four weeks ago, Miss Golonowska got tired of work, and felt she wanted a holiday; first being upset about her father's death, and then having a touch of malaria naturally took it out of her, and I rather sympathised with her wanting to get home; but as she wanted to go just before we had the final burst of finishing up we had to do this fortnight, I think I should have asked her to stay on that length of time, if she hadn't got to the stage when she was utterly useless. What annoyed me a little was that she had sufficient energy to stay up till all hours of the night talking, and to roam miles out into the villages visiting the people Miss Wrzeszcz had got to know. However Miss Wrzeszcz undertook to stay on and try and manage to get through, unless it happened that she got a post after the first fortnight in July. But she had no idea of doing more than the minimum. She started with a Roman Catholic holiday (when it is a sin to work) for which by the way Miss Golonowska stayed on, having already stayed on over the weekend, and promptly left off work at four every afternoon, no matter what she was in the middle of, and as there was a great deal to do and she works very slowly, I found we should have to spread things over into another week.

Now this morning she springs it on me that she intends going tomorrow, - implying that some job depended on it, - but Miss Stankiewicz says it is because Jane repeated something to the effect of her being stupid, to her sister who passed it on in a letter yesterday. It really is a low down thing to do because there is a long day's bonus distribution to do tomorrow and it will mean that Miss Stankiewicz doing it instead of her, - and to go to Mass on Sunday is the greatest event in Miss Stankiewicz's week. However she is being fairly decent about it. She however is on the verge of striking because she can't have her whole months holiday in one go (she isn't entitled to a month until next Xmas) and because she doesn't think she is getting a sufficient holiday maintenance allowance, - and I'm to pursue Jane to England with enquiries about same.

The work we have been doing has consisted of calculating the wages of each woman for the whole year, taking a percentage, calculating the amount and value of work from each village not returned from last year, collecting a flat sum from the bonus of each village to pay for it, - endeavouring to track and get in all of this year's outstanding work, and making lists for the Soltys and getting them to hunt up last year's. There are pounds and pounds worth of stuff out from last year, but if you try to investigate you don't get anywhere; either the woman is dead, or has moved, to another village; or she swears black and blue that she did not take any work, - or if she took it, that she returned it. Many of them say the same about work that has not been checked as being given in this year, and really one has to accept it, because the other two do the cards when I am not there and are hopelessly inaccurate (which rather sounds as though I consider myself infallible, - but what I mean is that I can either remember or not remember a woman coming in if she reminds me of some special circumstance, but I can't answer for the other two, and I can't say that they never make a mistake, and that therefore what is on the card must be correct.)

Then there have been the actual visits to pay the bonus; you can only do one or two in the day, and it takes a great deal of time; it is uneconomical from anything but the point of view of moral effect to go round to the villages instead of getting the women to come in, and it won't be seen until next year whether the moral effect was sufficient for it to be worth it. It is of course interesting to see the different villages, and we have really been rather lucky about the weather. One day particularly we were on the edge of a tremendous storm (with a furmanka breakdown into the bargain) but we escaped it.

Yesterday, for an exception was truly heavenly. We had a distribution, or rather a collecting of work at Drohiczyn the day before, and I slept the night outside, and woke to a gloriously sunny day; I got up at five, - Miss Wrzeszcz had been up since four to finish Quo Vadis which she is re-reading for the 6th time, we had breakfast, finished off some lists, prepared sandwiches, and started off at 9 in a funny little peasant furmanka with basket sides. The first village was Nahorige, quite near, - just a cluster of huts the other side of the railway. It isn't big enough to have a Soltys so we called on the Djieciatne, a man who has ten men or more under him, and gave him our list of people; there were several who hadn't brought work back; some were found and made the usual excuses, and some from this year returned theirs; then just as we had finished paying the bonus there was a tremendous excitement, some bees swarmed over our heads, some women came running out with branches and yelling, till out of every house some one or other burst forth with a branch and joined them in their chase. They run after the bees to prevent them settling on any person or animal. As if they did, they would sting them to death.

We drove out of Nahorige through cornfields; the corn is nearly ripe and people began to take advantage of the fine weather to start reaping. The first peasant we saw cut a swathe, and running towards the furmanka, bound it round each of our waists, wishing us all the luck for the coming year; it's an old custom, and you are supposed to return something more tangible than good wishes. They have all sorts of such customs for after harvest; when the first bread is made it is taken in a new handkerchief to the owner of the land from which the corn was taken.

Our furman called at his home for a scythe with which to cut food for his horse and fixed it along the side like a punt pole, and then we set off in real earnest. There are no roads as you know, we follow tracks across the marshes where logs were once laid down, but they are in a terrible state with holes more than a foot deep, and ruts and mud or dust; you get tossed up and down, shaken from side to side, and wonder you are not in pieces when at last you stop; the seat which is made of hay invariably sinks in the middle with a tilt which pitches you forward or off the back, or else throws you at your companion in the middle; all the scenery is very much the same, - a bit march, then fields of corn, flax, or a kind of vetch, - but the sky, especially on stormy days, with low rolling clouds gives it variety; here and there is a village, a windmill or a cluster of baby birches; and at Drohiczyn there is a line of low forest land bounding one part of the horizon.

Zawieliewie was a village where we have a hundred workers or so, and a young and energetic Soltys set off to find the women who hadn't given back work; meanwhile we paid those who had. Some seemed pleased, - but hardly anyone says thank you, - other began the "I took work more times than she did and haven't got as much" stunt, - most were quite impassive. All sorts of villagers come and stand round and stare, and continue to stare whatever question you ask them, without replying. It took us two or three hours from start to finish here, the Soltys evidently had a hot time trying to get the women to return last year's work and arrived back in an exhausted state quite incapable of taking in anything about a muddle with three women called Alexandra Wasiuk; when these people do talk they do it all together and the women particularly are no respecters of persons of authority.

We had our lunch at the corner of a cornfield, in sight of a cluster of pines which are always planted round grave yards here, - goodness knows why, -

Miniature adults. *Margaret was surprised that Belorussian children dressed in the same fashion as adults, rather than in 'children's' clothes as they would have in England.*

and would have loved to have stayed there all afternoon, it was so peaceful and beautiful. At the next village, Brassewicze things went somewhat faster; we had already been there once to look up the delinquents. Several people who had worked in previous years but not last year came to swell the crowd of envious admirers; the village dressmaker, a cripple, was among them and she passed her hand across Miss Wrzeszcz's frock and my jumper to examine how they were made; they were all very amused to see that Miss Wrzeszcz hadn't their own amount of muscle, and when I shewed them my skinny arm they simply roared as though it was the best joke they had met for a long time. They are all dressed in fairly long skirts, a kind of shirt blouse generally and a linen apron, all of these things more or less embroidered according to the greatness of the occasion; they all wear head handkerchiefs, - generally white, tied under their chins; they think it is immodest to show their hair, - and if they have work that needs short skirts they bind their legs round with material – it looks like long drawers beneath their skirts. On the other hand they think nothing of their blouses with nothing on underneath gaping two inches from neck to waist. Such is modesty! In the remoter villages all the small children, right down to the babies almost are diminutive replicas of the grown ups; little girls with frocks to their ankles and boys with trousers; since we started bonusing I have begun to realize how very urban Horodec is after all.

Our money was beginning to give out, - it had been impossible to calculate before leaving Horodec how much we should need, and I had brought everything I could get changed, - so the next village having stolen an appalling lot of work last year we simple left the list to the head man, and departed amid the curses of the multitude.

Cypki and Plissesyce only had a few each, and at five or so we set our faces homeward. I had promised to go out and see the Wyslouchs who had very kindly lent us horses earlier in the week. Another of the sons is home at the moment from Vilna University where he is studying law and economics. They are the only interesting Polish family I have met. This one is a pacifist, though his other brother is taking up the army as a career; he has been all through the war here, and is now taking up the study of government because he says no one knows anything about it in Poland, and people need to build up something decent in the way of a state; he is very interested in Labour in England. He amuses me awfully because he is such a mixture of youthful student and quite experienced man, - is frightfully definite in his opinions and never stops talking to take breath even. But it's all his own, thought out, which makes him interesting. I only had time to say 'How do you do' and come away, but he raced to the station too, talking all the time.

As you might imagine our housing problem continues to viscitate [sic]. We have to give this up at the end of August unless we buy it; the new Priest followed in the footsteps of the old by refusing to let us remove our own wash house after giving his promised word, and by trying to screw out of us a carpet worth 125 zl. when he was only entitled to 80 zl.

Tomorrow is Wednesday and Thursday there will be more bonus work; on Friday Miss Stankiewicz will depart, and I shall be left alone to cope with all the work that has come in, the remaining loom room, the bonus accounts, the housekeeping (which won't be much) and all the general clearing up. I had hoped to have things ship shape for my successor but it looks as though I shall have to wait until she comes to get on with the stock taking part of the tidying up. I also intended composing a book of hints, - that may still get done, - in all the various branches of the works and starting with a few general axioms. Such as for example:

> Having been given the problem of cutting out a
> pattern equal to a give pattern ever so many times,
> it is invariably necessary to measure one with the
> other. For either the first will be longer than the
> second, or the second will be narrower than the
> first. Otherwise they would both be equal in length
> and breadth, which, given a Polish cutter is absurd.
>
> Taking any number of tea sets, bridge sets or
> luncheon sets, no set is ever found in which all the
> square, after having been given out are equal to the
> given square, etc. etc.

My successor is Hilda Buckmaster; I don't know much about her except that she has been working for the National Union of Students, has already some Polish friends and has been told all the disadvantages of the job, and is still keen; she is probably coming out on the 10th, and we shall come back here immediately together, - I shall be in Warsaw from the 1st. Anybody writing between July 26th and August 6th please address letters to K.P.P.K.W., Widok 26.

And EIGHT WEEKS TODAY I SHALL BE HOME!!!!!!! I am starting seven weeks tomorrow but am spending the inside of a week in Belgium on the way, - where I am not quite sure. I expect this will be the last journal unless I write from Warsaw; it will depend whether anything worth relating turns up. If not farewell until glorious September when I hope to see at least six of your number if not more!

Much love, Margaret.

xx xxx xx

Henry Harris, Dr Lucy Harris and Hilda Buckmaster, August 1925. Margaret made her final visit to Horodec in August to introduce her replacement Hilda to the work of the project, and to help the new head of the Warsaw Unit, Henry Harris, to negotiate new leases for premises for the project.

Antoni Izydor Wyslouch (1864–1940) The Wyslouchs were an aristocratic family of Polish-Lithuanian descent who owned several estates including one at Pirkowicze near Drohiczyn. The family had a long tradition of involvement in politics and public life, and in the 19th century they supported education for and the emancipation of the lower classes. During World War One they suffered considerable property damage, but as Poles they were returned to their former position in the ruling classes. With the return to power of Pilsudski in 1926 their expectations rose. Boleslaw Wyslouch became a senator and founded the Polish People's Party. Anton was a historian and spoke fluent French, and in the 1930s became a member of the Polish parliament. The family's fortunes took a downturn with the Soviet invasion of 1940 and Anton was hung from a tree in his orchard. The Wyslouch's estate house at Pirkowicze is now used as a local school. [32]

Hilda Buckmaster (1887–1993) Hilda was born in London and raised an Anglican. In 1914, at the age of 17 she volunteered with the Red Cross and then in 1919 joined the Women's Royal Navy Service (WRNS) and worked as a motor mechanic and driver until 1919. In 1924 she graduated from the London School of Economics, with a degree in Economics and Public Administration and was sent by the government to Germany to study municipal affairs. She worked for the Council for International Service in Horodec for 18 months in 1925–26. After Poland she travelled widely, studied for a PhD at LSE in 1930–32, spent time as a deckhand on a sailing ship, and ran for parliament (unsuccessfully) three times. During World War Two she joined the WRNS again and rose to be Chief Officer. After the war she became the warden of a London university women's residence, and then, after immigrating to Canada in 1954, worked at the University of Toronto and the United Church Training School. She retired in 1972 and lived in Kingston until her death at 96. In 1965 Margaret sent Hilda these letters, and in 1980 Hilda passed them on to Margaret's great-nieces. [33]

xx xxx xx

This is the end of the collection of Margaret's journal letters. She continued to work on the project through the summer of 1925. She came to Warsaw at the end of July, but was back in Horodec in mid-August with Henry Harris negotiating about premises and introducing Hilda to the project. On 29 August she left Warsaw for Brussels where she spent a few days before returning to England.

Epilogue

What happened to these people afterwards? Many of the international staff continued to be involved in international humanitarian work and worked for social justice in their own countries. Margaret went home to continue her teaching career, but she was bitten by the travel bug, and worked again internationally for long periods during the rest of her life. In 1945 she worked again with the Friends helping refugees after World War Two in France, Austria and Germany.

The Women's Industries' embroidery project continued to function until 1937. In 1929 the work was handed over to a pair of dedicated Polish women who set up a new Polish organisation to continue the local work, while the Friends in England continued to take care of marketing the products internationally. The centre at Horodec was closed at this

Mother and son, Africa, c.1932. *Margaret with her son John who she adopted in 1929. She took him with her to Northern Rhodesia (Zambia) where she was headmistress of the Choma Beit School between 1931 and 1934.*

A life long correspondent. *Margaret at her writing desk in the 1950s.*

time and the work managed from Warsaw. The embroidery business continued to have strong sales for a couple of years, but as the international depression took hold in 1931 sales dropped off and the industry ran at a loss for the next seven years, buffered slightly by fluctuating exchange rates. The scale of distributions had to be reduced and after the death of one of the Polish sponsors in 1936 the project was forced to close completely in 1937.

The project had lasted 17 years from 1921 through to 1937, and had grown in the first four years from just 15 women participants to almost 5,000. Between 1923 and 1938 the project earned £25,000 which was ploughed back into wages for the women, and some charitable donations to their communities. More than a quarter of a million pieces of embroidered work were sold in England alone for nearly £43,000.

In 1939 war came again to the province of Polesia. Many of the Belarusian peasants who had struggled to rebuild their lives with the support of this project, lost everything again, became refugees again, and many died. The Friends, through the auspices of the AFSC and the Friends Service Council (the successor organization to the CIS), built on the lessons they learned from their work in post-World War One Europe. They continued with their mission to provide relief to the victims of man's inhumanity to man, but their ability to help the Belarusian peasants during World War Two was limited by the scale of that war. In 1947 the two organizations were awarded the Nobel Peace Prize. The Friends' organizations continue their work in humanitarian aid and carry on a tradition of providing innovative examples of constructive peacemaking to the aid community to this day.

Map

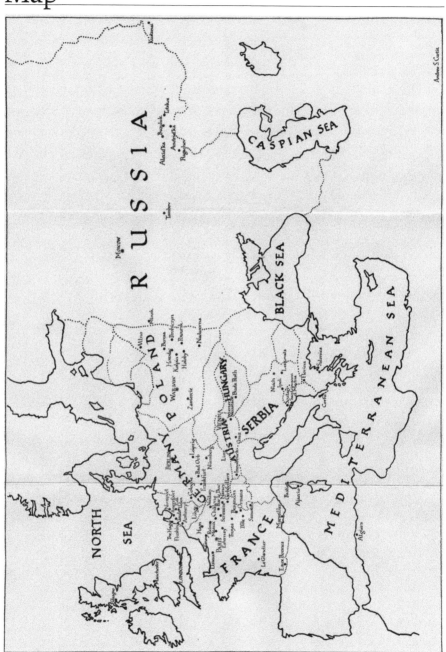

Map showing the Principal Centres of the Friends' Relief Work in Europe, 1914–23, from
A Quaker Adventure, by A. Ruth Fry, 1926. [14]

Acknowledgements

The genesis of this book was the gift of a package containing the letters, a photograph album and additional contemporary project documents, from Hilda Buckmaster to Margaret's great-niece and my sister Sarah Cooper in 1981. Hilda was an old friend and relief work colleague of Margaret's, and Margaret sent her the letters in 1964.

A number of people provided valuable assistance with research in the preparation of this work. Joseph Keith, at the Library of the Religious Society of Friends, Friends House, London, gave generous assistance and advice with archival research about the Quaker's work in Poland and Margaret's role it. The original letters now reside in this library. Lyndon S. Back shared her experience of researching and writing about American Quaker volunteers in Poland during the same time. Dr. Johannes Paulmann, of the University of Mannheim, was kind enough to allow me to attend the 2011 conference on Dilemmas of International Aid in the Twentieth Century at the German Historical Institute in London where I gained a wider perspective on current academic research on the history of humanitarian aid. Davide Rodogno, Shaloma Gauthier, and Francesca Piana, shared their paper on humanitarian aid in Poland in the post-World War One period and their experience with archival research on this topic. Hannah Kadmon, project coordinator for the translation of the Horodetz Yizkor book, within the Yizkor Book Project at JewishGen.org has given permission to quote from that book here. Erling Kjekstad provided information about how his father came to be working with the Quakers in Poland in the 1920s. Heather Nisbet and Kathy Kelsey helped with proof-reading and gave valuable editing suggestions.

Note on transcription

This document is based on 13 letters written for circulation to a specific list of friends, most of which were typed, and two hand written drafts of similar letters written for a presentation to a more general audience. The 13 letters which comprise the 'journal' are presented in their entirety in the order they were written. Paragraphs from the two general letters have been excerpted throughout the introductory chapters, and are not presented in the order they were written. In some cases sentences and paragraphs from both letters have been combined into one section.

[Square brackets] have been used for all words and names inserted in the text by the editor for clarification All text in (round brackets) is from the original documents. Spelling of Polish personal and geographic names has been standardised, but the correct Polish fonts are not supported for most eReaders. The original letters were typed on an English typewriter which did not have Polish letters. Many of the places in the letters are now known by Belarusian names rather than the Polish names used in the 1920s which makes locating them on a modern map a challenge and choosing one 'correct' spelling impossible. Likewise, some people's names are difficult to render into English. For instance, the loom girl who lives with Margaret is referred to in Margaret's original letters as Weira, and in other Friends' publications as Vera, but if she had written her name herself she probably would have spelled it in Cyrillic. All references to the first Miss Wrzeszcz have been rendered as Sophia Wrzeszcz to distinguish her from her sister, who is also Miss Wrzeszcz.

Some minor changes to punctuation have been made for clarity of reading, but the majority of the punctuation is from the original letters. Obvious typing errors have been corrected, and handwritten corrections made by Margaret on the typed originals have been inserted without comment. A few archaic spellings have been changed, e.g. Margaret used shew for show in some cases. In a few cases Margaret's longer paragraphs have been divided for ease of reading.

References

1. Ben-Ezra, A., ed. Horodetz: History of a Town, 1142 – 1942 (Gorodets, Belarus). Translation of Horodets; a geshikhte fun a shtetl, 1142 – 1942. 1949, www.jewishgen.org: New York.

2. Polish Research Centre, Eastern Poland. 1941, Polish Research Centre London.

3. Warshawsky, D., ed. Drohiczn; 500 years of Jewish life. Translation of Drohiczyn; finf hundert yor yidish lebn. 1958, Book Committee Drohichyn: Chicago.

4. Hamilton, H.W., The Aftermath of War: Experiences of a Quaker Relief Officer on the Polish-Russian Border 1923–1924. 1982, Dayton, Ohio: Morningside House, Inc.

5. Esposito, B.G.V.J., ed. The West Point Atlas of War: World War 1. 1995, Black Dog & Leventhal Publishers Inc.: New York.

6. Beeuwkes, H., American Medical and Sanitary Relief in the Russian Famine, 1921–1923. ~1924, American Relief Administration: New York.

7. Dandelion, B.P., The Quakers: A Very Short Introduction. 2008, Oxford: Oxford University Press.

8. Scott, R.C., Quakers in Russia. 1964, London: Michael Joseph.

9. Five Million Face Famine in Poland, in The New York Times. 1919, The New York Times: New York.

10. ARA, A brief description of the work conducted in Poland by the American Relief Administration in cooperation with the Polish government. Krotki zarys Dziaalnosci amerykanskiego wydziau ratunkowego prowadzonej przy wspóludziale rzadu polskiego na terenie rzeczypospolitej polskie. 1922, American Relief Administration: New York.

11. Jones, L., Quakers in Action: Recent Humanitarian and Reform Activities of the American Quakers. 1929, New York: The MacMillan Company.

12. Gauthier, S., F. Piana, and D. Rodogno, Shaping Poland: Relief and Rehabilitation Programmes Undertaken by Foreign Organizations, 1918–1922, in From Relief to Rehabilitation. Transnational Humanitarian Actions in the Aftermath of the First World War (1918–1933). 2001, Graduate Institute of International and Development Studies: Geneva.

13. Back, L.S., Rebecca Janney Timbres Clark: Turned in the Hand of God, in Pendle Hill Pamphlet. 2007, Pendle Hill Publications: Wallingford, PA.

14. Fry, A.R., A Quaker Adventure: The Story of Nine Years' Relief and Reconstruction. 1926, London: Nisbet & Co. Ltd.

15. Haberman, F.W., ed. Nobel Lectures, Peace 1926–1950. 1972, Elsevier Publishing Company: Amsterdam.

16. AFSC. AFSC History. n.d. [cited 2011 January 23]; Available from: http://afsc.org/afsc-history.

17. Jordan, A., Polish Peasant Handicrafts: An Account of the Polish Industries Work 1919–1939. 1941, Friends Service Council: London.

18. Watt, R.M., Bitter Glory: Poland and Its Fate 1918 to 1939. 1979, New York: Simon and Schuster.

19. Hicks, J. and G. Allen, A Century of Change: Trends in UK statistics since 1900, in Research Paper 99/11. 1999, House of Commons: London.

20. Oldfield, S., Compiling the First Dictionary of British Women Humanitarians – Why? What? Who? How/. Women's Studies International Forum, 2001. 24(6): p. 737-743.

21. Riley, N.D., Heinrich Ernst Karl Jordan. 1861–1959. Biographical Memoirs of Fellows of the Royal Society, 1960. 6(Nove 1960): p. 106–133.

22. Friends Library, Collection of manuscript biographies of prominent Quakers. n.d., Friends Library: London.

23. Young, W., Visible Witness: A Testimony for Radical Peace Action. 1961, Pendle Hill Publications: Wallingford, PA.

24. Pendle Hill, Index of Pendle Hill Pamphlets. 2010, Pendle Hill Publications: Wallingford, PA.

25. Bremner, J. (1983) Heagney, Muriel Agnes (1885 – 1974). Australian Dictionary of Biography Online.

26. Francis, R., Chapter 3: Famine relief on the Volga, Muriel Heagney's winter sojourn, in Political Tourists, Melbourne University Press: Melbourne.

27. Lerski, G., Herbert Hoover and Poland: A Documentary History of Friendship. 1977, Stanford, CA: Hoover Institution Press.

28. Kjekstad, E., About Erline Kjekstad. 2011: Olso, Norway.

29. McFadden, D. and C. Gorfinkel, Constructive Spirit: Quakers in Revolutionary Russia. 2004, Pasadena, CA: Intentional Productions.

30. Oldfield, S., Barrow, Florence Mary, in Oxford National Dictionary of Biography, L. Goldman, Editor. 2011, Oxford University Press: Oxford.

31. Zamoyski, A., Warsaw 1920: Lenin's Failed Conquest of Europe. 2008, London: HaperCollinsPublishers.

32. Coleman, A.P. and M.M. Coleman, Books and Things. 1970, Cherry Hill Books: Cheshire, Connecticut

33. Hidla Buckmaster – Obituray. 1993, Personal collection: Kingston.

ND - #0323 - 270225 - C0 - 234/156/10 - PB - 9781780911434 - Gloss Lamination